**Fresh Praise**

"Michael D. Brown's 6.5 Fresh Steps for delivering a world-class customer service experience are truly fresh and right on! It's a salad bar of fresh ideas for enhancing that most important experience... that experience the customer has with you and your business. "

—Sam Allman, Speaker, Consultant, and Entrepreneur
Author of *Heart and Mind Selling: The New Secret to Closing the Sale and Winning the Customer for Life*

"Fresh Customer Service is a wonderful resource that helps managers and leaders change their priorities to keep business booming. I would recommend it to anyone who works with a staff under him."

—Calvin Mackie, Ph.D.
Author of *A View from the Roof—Lessons for Life & Business*

"Until reading Michael D. Brown's Fresh Customer Service I had no idea how much placing the customer ahead of the employees was damaging the bottom line. I am confident that if businesses adopt Michael's strategies, profits, customer loyalty, and workplace morale will all increase dramatically."

—John Napolitano CPA, CFP, PFF
Chairman and CEO of US Wealth Management, LLC

"Michael D. Brown is a man on a mission. This book will transform your customer service experience. If you want first class results then you need to read this book and then share it with everyone you know. It will change their lives."

"Michael D. Brown's new book, *Fresh Customer Service*, outlines a brilliant, hands-on approach for customer service. Not a theoretical book, it presents concrete, proven examples that are working in today's time-sensitive, high-stress customer driven environments. These practices show that customer service can be transformed from pretty posters on the wall to efficient and effective actions on the frontline. All industries should be looking at these fresh breakthrough concepts."

"Michael's concepts are real and the results are proven everyday in top companies across America. It really is about the frontline employee—they are the ones that touch your customers every day. Michael's 6.5 Fresh Steps put the focus where it should be—on the employee!"

"Refreshing (pardon the pun) is the word I'd choose to describe this new book on customer service.

So many have written on this subject and said pretty much the same, but Michael D. Brown has actually found a new and practical approach to this well traveled topic. He says we should focus first on our employees and second on our customers. I agree. When we start treating the caregivers with the care we want them to give, then we get loyal, happy and profitable customers."

—**Jim Cathcart, author of** *Relationship Selling, The Eight Competencies of Top Sales Producers*

"A 'must-read' for any frontline manager. Michael D. Brown provides great clarity into why it is important to treat the employee as #1. His insight is truly refreshing but also spot on."

—**Ian D. Bishop, ChFC CMFC**
Branch Manager, Ameriprise Financial
(An American Express Company)

Fresh
CUSTOMER SERVICE

Fresh

CUSTOMER SERVICE

TREAT **THE EMPLOYEE AS #1** AND
THE CUSTOMER AS #2 AND YOU WILL
GET CUSTOMERS FOR LIFE

BY MICHAEL D. BROWN, MBA

Boston, Massachusetts
www.AcanthusPublishing.com

Published by Acanthus Publishing
a division of The Ictus Group, LLC
343 Commercial St
Unit 214, Union Wharf
Boston, MA 02109

Printed in the United States of America
10 9 8 7 6 5 4 3 2 1

Publisher's Cataloging-In-Publication Data
(Prepared by The Donohue Group, Inc.)

Brown, Michael D., 1972-
  Fresh customer service: Treat the employee as #1 and the customer as #2 and you will get
customers for life / by Michael D. Brown, MBA.

   p. : ill. ; cm.

   ISBN: 978-1-933631-64-6

1. Customer services. 2. Service industries workers--Training of. 3. Success in business. I.
Title.
HF5415.5 .B769 2007
658.8/12

Cover design and interior layout by Sarah Martin
Edited by Carolyn Holliday McKibbin

This book is dedicated to my mother,
my ten brothers and sisters, and the
hundreds of people who have worked for
and with me over the last 20 years.

Thank You!

Table of Contents

Foreword
by Keith E. Ayers

We have all experienced bad service in restaurants, hotels, airplanes, and retail stores, where the staff do little to disguise their apathy toward us, the customer. Even in places where you would think you might get a few kind words and empathy when you're sick or injured, like the hospital emergency room, physicians and hospital staff seem too busy and distracted to care about *our* problems.

And yet you would be hard-pressed to find a business leader or physician who would argue that they don't want their staff to provide great service. Leaders don't intentionally set out to create policies and procedures that will upset their customers enough that they will leave and go to a competitor.

Unfortunately, too many leaders think the solution to improving customer service is to invest in technology. So, we have more sophisticated phone answering systems that make it more difficult, and in some cases impossible, to talk with a live person.

Michael D. Brown has hit the nail on the head with his hook: *The employee is number one, not the customer. The customer is number two.*

Herb Kelleher, former CEO and Founder of Southwest Airlines, established the same principle as a foundation of the organization's culture. He knew that if the company took good care of its employees, the employees would take good care of the customers. Satisfied customers not only come back, they bring their friends and family with them. Herb understood that Southwest's *customers would never be treated better than their employees.*

The Gallup Organization research reinforces this point with a strong correlation between *employee engagement* and *customer engagement.* Highly engaged employees create highly engaged, loyal customers.

Michael came to this same conclusion, that the employee is number one, as a result of his own life experience. His stories about his early years as a Frontline Employee and the lessons he learned from his customers, co-workers, and managers make this book easy and fun to read. But it also packs a powerful punch.

The principles in *Fresh Customer Service* need to be applied by your Frontline Employees, but they won't want to and won't be able to unless you read and apply the principles first. Treating employees as number one, truly valuing and respecting them, must start from the top of the organization, and must be applied by every manager and supervisor if you really want to provide world class service. The reason so few organizations successfully do this is that they don't have a system in place for ensuring that all employees are trusted and treated with respect.

What Michael provides you in this book is a foundational system to put in place to guarantee your employees give *World-Class* customer service every time. It is more like an *operating system* than a program. Microsoft Word® and PowerPoint® don't work at all without the Microsoft Windows® operating system. Your Customer Relations Management (CRM) program won't work at improving customer service unless you have the *people operating system* in place.

That is what Fresh Customer Service is—*a customer service operating system* that provides the systems and foundational knowledge and skills employees need to provide *World-Class* service every time. And very few people would disagree with me that World-Class service is lacking in many organizations today.

When I first started out as a consultant 30 years ago in my home country of Australia, I used to travel to the United States at least once a year to attend conferences and learn from the best in my field. I remember thinking how great the service was here in the US compared to Australia at that time… and it was good. Certainly better than it is today. The standard seems to have slipped significantly.

As an international consultant I have worked with hundreds of companies and thousands of leaders, and I don't remember many who didn't want to trust their employees to be more accountable. At the same time, most leaders fear letting go of control. They believe that some employees would take advantage of the system. Michael's systems, in particular **Make-It-Right Power** and the **What-If Arsenal**, provide leaders with practical tools they can use to trust Frontline Employees to solve customer problems and make sound decisions.

The long term success of your organization is very dependent on relationships: the relationship each employee has with his or her immediate manager, and the relationships each employee has with your customers. The 6.5 steps to Fresh Customer Service will give you the systems to put in place to maximize these relationships and the financial success of your organization.

A final word about the author. Michael has been on an incredible journey since his humble beginnings on the "wrong" side of the tracks in Mississippi. His compassion for people, his drive to do his best in everything he did, and his hunger to learn how to be better, have all contributed to his successful career. He is also pretty smart. He has figured out from his own experiences what it takes to build a great organization that earns the commitment and loyalty of both employees and customers. And from my experience, he is right on the money.

Keith E. Ayers
President, Integro Leadership Institute LLC
West Chester, PA
Author of *Engagement Is Not Enough—*
You Need Passionate Employees to Achieve Your Dream
(Advantage October 2006)
www.EngagementIsNotEnough.com

Preface

I have been on the frontline of customer service for almost my entire life. It all started in fourth grade back in Holmes County, Mississippi, when I took a job working as a handyman and housecleaner for a wealthy lady living on the "right" side of the tracks, whom I will call Norma.

Providing customer service to Norma was not an easy task by any means. Norma felt that her social position entitled her to be crotchety and demanding, as well as physically violent if her every whim was not fulfilled. I have to admit that at times she could be very accommodating, but this friendly demeanor was usually part of some elaborate mind game she would play to keep me from getting too comfortable. And the harder I worked, the more she demanded. Every day I walked on eggshells.

This notion of "walking on eggshells" is the perfect lead-in to a story that exemplifies the Frontline Employee environment Norma created for me. It all started one Saturday morning when I was cooking breakfast (by this point I was tall enough to reach the stove). Normally, she wanted her eggs "hard," but I never knew exactly what she meant by "hard." Just how hard was "hard" supposed to be? It seemed like I never got it right. But on this particular Saturday, I thought I had it down pat. Imagine my surprise when she screamed, "You just don't get it. You should know by now."

I carefully explained that the eggs were cooked the same way they had been the previous weekend, when she appeared to like them. Norma took this as license to raise her hand and shove me in the chest. "Don't talk back to me like that," she said. Prior to this incident, I had never talked back to her. And I wasn't even trying to "talk back" so much as I was merely attempting to understand why she was upset with the eggs when she had liked them the week before. After she pushed me, I walked away.

The next weekend, she led me to believe things were fine. She was being agreeable, but I never knew how she would react to any given situation. And I don't think I ever did get the eggs right!

In a classic example of Norma's mind games, after the egg incident she eased up on her criticism of my cooking skills, but shortly after she moved on to criticizing how I cleaned the glass and mirrors in her house. I always used too much or too little glass cleaner. She never stopped finding something new to keep me on edge.

Norma knew I was a perfectionist, and I think she reasoned, "I'll always tell him he's not doing it right; that way he'll work harder." To make matters worse, when I didn't respond the first time she shoved me, it became a license for her to push me around even more.

This unpleasant situation offered me two choices: Stick it out or leave.

As one of ten siblings being raised by my widowed mother, living in the fourth-poorest county in the country, leaving did not appear to be a viable option. Despite the many hardships, I enjoyed and needed this job's financial compensation. So I grinned and bore it, swallowing all the pride a nine-year-old boy could have. But after two years of slaving away for Norma, finally I decided to escape.

Every summer, there was an exchange trip where students from our rural Mississippi county would live with a family in Wisconsin for four to six weeks and a child from that family would come to live in Mississippi. The summer after the egg incident, I wanted to go on this trip, but hadn't scheduled it because Norma had forbidden me, saying it would take me away from my work. The bus was set to leave on a Saturday and the Friday before it departed, there was a cancellation on the trip. I asked my mother if I could go and she agreed. That Saturday morning, I got on that bus and rode away from Norma and my job!

When I got back in August, there was a note for me saying Norma had a bike waiting for me at her house. Naturally, this was another one of her little mind games she had devised to manipulate me. When I got there, there was no bike, but Norma started in on me, saying, "Why would you leave? I was so good to you. You won't be anything without me. I'm all you have financially. I can help you with your schooling."

I fell for Norma's tricks and manipulations one last time. I agreed to return and try the job out again for a week. She went right back to her old behavior of mistreating me. By the third day, I knew I needed to get out of there. So I ran like hell and never went back!

A lady in my church, Mrs. Moses, had offered me free piano lessons, which Norma had prohibited me from accepting since they would distract me from my job. After running away, I took Mrs. Moses up on her offer and moved from working to focusing on school (although I had managed to maintain high grades during the entire experience with Norma) and piano lessons.

As brutal as the experience with Norma had been, it was not without its lessons. I learned that using fear isn't an ideal way to treat employees; strict authority is damaging to their morale, self-esteem, and self-confidence. I also learned that setting clear expectations, providing feedback (be it good or bad), the occasional "thank you," and mutual respect must be the foundation of an employee-employer relationship.

In addition, working for Norma taught me to never give up on satisfying the customer. I needed to deliver a service to her, and when she told me it wasn't right, it affected me. I began doubting myself. But now I realize that sometimes, as it was with Norma, it will never be right. You have to understand people and what makes them happy. You need to realize that while sometimes a problem is just a result of a customer's personality, you can still continue to try hard to satisfy them and take their feedback.

Above all, though, I learned that **human beings don't embrace fear; they run from it**. Look at how I ran from Norma! Using fear as a motivator to drive results will probably achieve short-term gains, but not *sustainable* gains. All fear produces in the long term are employees who run away from you and your organization.

Later in my frontline career, I found myself flipping burgers at a popular fast food joint while I was getting my undergraduate degree in management at Jackson State University. Here I learned a very different lesson. I originally applied to fill an advertised cashier opening, but the general manager told me they really needed someone to work the grill. Even though I had previous cashier experience and great references, not to mention *I was currently studying management at Jackson State University*, I still wasn't considered a viable candidate for the cashier position. So the managers hid me back in the kitchen.

Although my title was officially "burger-flipper/grillman," it soon became much more. Sure, I worked the grill for four months, which was a hot, sweaty, and grueling job. But I was also the onsite therapist/coach—motivating employees after a manager's scolding, turning their tears into a tenacity to serve customers and get the job done. I drove immense results, cutting wait time at the drive-through window from two minutes and thirty seconds to one minute and twenty seconds. It was teamwork "Michael D. Brown style," and the employees loved it. Yet despite my results and the love the whole staff had for me, it was many months before I finally got promoted to cashier.

I soon figured out from a conversation initiated by the general manager that my qualifications, or lack thereof, had nothing to do with why I hadn't been offered the cashier position earlier. According to the general manager, the regional manager had told him that he didn't want to see black people as cashiers at the front counter waiting on customers because the restaurant was located in an affluent area.

Since then, I have always tried to overcompensate my actions due to obvious and camouflaged racism. As a result of this experience and others like it, I couldn't escape the thought that I had to do much better than anyone else. My intense focus on the frontline that generated results and outputs which beat expectations helped me climb the corporate ladder, because no one in the organizations, firms, or corporations I worked at could deny the results. I kept attention off myself (and my skin color) by delivering better than anyone else and building a professional "cushion" for myself.

These two early frontline customer service experiences had a tremendous impact on both my personal worldview and on how I conduct myself professionally. But a third early frontline customer service experience, this one taking place when I was twenty-two years old, really set me on the path that has led me to where I am today. In fact, I often joke that a dime changed my life.

One day, I was helping a Frontline Employee count down his cash drawer. I was the multi-unit manager at an international airport. I counted out the dimes and ended up with thirty-four. As I wrote $3.40 on the balance sheet, my boss, Roy, walked by and asked me *how* I was counting the dimes. I told him that I just counted the number of dimes and multiplied the sum by ten.

"That's not the way I want you to count the dimes!" Roy yelled. "Let me show you how to do it. You have to put the dimes in stacks of ten so that each stack equals one dollar."

I said, "Well, it looks like we got the same total, even though we used different counting methods."

In a fiery voice, Roy replied, "I'm going to write you up for being insubordinate!"

With those stacks of dimes reflecting in my eye and Roy finding yet another way to let me know I was inferior to him —he had given me about 10 other examples prior to this incident—I had an epiphany. Roy's aggression was making my temperature rise, and I suddenly realized I just wasn't going to take it anymore. It's funny that something as insignificant as how one counts dimes can be the straw that breaks the camel's back.

Just like with Norma many years earlier, it was my time to run. Though I had received praise for increasing sales, driving down employee turnover, and improving customer satisfaction scores, it was time for me to move on with the remaining shreds of dignity I had. In leaving this job, I took my life and my career into my own hands.

I've come a long way since. I've spent time working on the frontlines, consulting with customer service managers, business unit leaders, directors, department heads, regional managers, and frontline managers in a diverse set of companies, organizations, and industries. Physically, I left the frontline behind. But I have since been able to successfully infuse my learnings and detailed understanding of the Frontline Employee into the various roles, responsibilities, and positions I have had at a number of companies and organizations, such as Murphy Oil (The Wal-Mart Project), USF&G Insurance, BP, Wells Fargo Financial, San Francisco Foundation, Ford Foundation, Amoco, Wendy's International, Ralph & Kacoo's, and a number of small independent business owners. I have been able to wow audiences as a spokesperson in corporate videos and live television appearances, and as a trainer, commentator, coach, lecturer, and keynote speaker. But it's thanks to my humble beginnings and background in burger-flipping, housecleaning, and waiting tables that I never lost my connection—mentally and emotionally—with the frontline worker. I'll never forget what it's like to be low man on the totem poll.

Throughout all my jobs, I've excelled at meeting and surpassing customer service standards. But my drive doesn't just come from my own experience on the frontlines. As a child, even before my job with Norma, I was exposed to work-related indignities that made a tremendous impression on me.

When I was a little boy in Mississippi, I used to watch as the owner of a nearby cotton plantation drove his big, dusty pick-up truck into town and offer neighborhood people cotton-picking jobs. Usually, about half a dozen people would jump on the back of the truck and be hauled off to the cotton field for the day. Then they'd return in the evening, dog tired and complaining of the grueling work, the hot sun, the pains in their hands and backs, and the poor pay.

I also watched as people awoke at three o'clock every morning to board a bus that would drive them two hours away to work in poultry factories. They would return late that evening, miserable, with the stench of chicken guts lingering long after they had bathed. The next day, they'd speak about how the factory managers would focus only on constant production and cared very little about them as human beings, despite the wet, slippery floor and that foul odor that congested the working facilities.

And, perhaps most vividly, I remember my mother coming home from a minimum wage job, physically and mentally exhausted and dreading the next workday. Our family was poor and she was our sole provider. She worked at a restaurant because she had to provide for her children, regardless of the environment that she had to work in.

From my surroundings and my experiences I absorbed my servant-leadership mentality—the belief that when the employee is taken care of first, he or she will take care of the customer in return. I've learned to work with the employee to create the customer experience. I equip and empower Frontline Employees with the tools necessary to deliver Fresh Customer Service. From here, a World-Class customer experience is possible and bottom line growth will inevitably follow.

Early in my professional career, I was bombarded with overly-prescriptive program initiatives, lofty sales goals, budget cuts, new competition, and more aggressive competitors. I initially started by simply executing the programs that were given to me. However, simple execution was only delivering marginal results. I knew I could do better. I knew that something was missing; something was preventing me from moving the business further, faster.

I tried pushing the various programs on the Frontline Employees. I tried the whip. I tried sugar coating. I tried baiting. I tried everything to get the Frontline Employees to take the programs and initiatives higher. Still, I wanted to do more—something fun and creative but still within the guidelines. I tried every program designed to increase employee participation, all to no avail.

But I noticed there was a loophole. Nowhere did it say that you couldn't motivate your employees by innovative means. Nothing said you couldn't present the offer in a more creative, team-oriented way.

There was also nothing that really detailed what I couldn't do to excite, motivate and equip Frontline Employees to a level where they could deliver a customer service experience that was World-Class and exceeded expectations. What I personally put in place and continued to refine throughout my career is Michael D. Brown's 6.5 Fresh Steps that will be presented in this book.

Now let me tell you, for most of my career I didn't have a formal name for these steps, nor did I consciously realize that there were 6.5. I've been questioned for years as to the secret of my success with leading people and delivering World-Class customer service. My typical response has always been that I believe in my Frontline Employees.

Needless to say, as time went on, people became hungrier for the process that I've been carrying in my head for several years. Consequently, I needed to organize my internal file cabinet and get the process on paper.... So now you have the 6.5 Fresh Steps to Fresh Customer Service.

I made a personal commitment to myself during my high school years that I wouldn't allow the typical correlation between poverty and failure to dictate my future. I dared to beat the odds by staying focused on my hopes, dreams, and aspirations. Within all of the Fortune 500 Companies, mid-sized organizations, and mom-and-pop stores for which I have worked, I have gone above and beyond simply executing programs and initiatives. I have wholeheartedly focused on the Frontline Employees—motivating them, preparing them, empowering them to deliver a World-Class experience.

At every company where I've worked, I have gotten the Frontline Employees to buy into and commit to delivering the very best customer service they can possibly offer. In each of these companies, I have been recognized for my commitment to employees and to the customers, and for achieving unprecedented bottom line results.

All this from a guy who grew up in rural Mississippi, a place that at the time of my youth was ranked at the bottom of almost all categories of national health standards. Statistically, there was a greater chance that I would struggle in my poverty-ridden county's cycle of destitution than I would achieve a successful career. The odds were against me becoming a highly successful business professional. Instead, I'd be a drug addict. Or an absent father. A criminal. But I beat the odds.

Now I am known by many of my colleagues, peers, friends, and Frontline Employees as a future-oriented, compassionate visionary. My use of personal, caring approaches and a supportive work environment where employees can exchange ideas and develop personal connections has given me credibility and trust among everyone I deal with. I am able to go several layers beneath any problem and propose fresh, sustainable solutions and robust strategies.

If you yearn to provide a World-Class customer service experience to your customers, read this Little Green Book. You can be proactive by reading this book or you can wait until you lose market share and are forced to shell out millions of dollars at a (perhaps futile) recovery attempt. This book does not contain failed complex theories on customer service or pseudo-customer service programs. Nor does this book contain complex formulas, trade secrets, or any other "proprietary" terminology that some so-called "experts" like to peddle. I have avoided all the stale hooey, opting for 6.5 Fresh Steps that deliver Fresh Customer Service. I have used real solutions that affect real people and deliver real results.

What you will find in the following pages is a professional who is passionate about people—Frontline Employees and customers. You will clearly see how by taking care of the Frontline Employee first, he or she will be better equipped and empowered to take care of your customers. That's right, **take care of the employee first**. I will expand upon this radical idea in the Introduction and throughout each of the 6.5 Fresh Steps.

The result of following my simple, battle-tested advice? A bottom line you never believed was possible. The 6.5 Fresh Steps and other ideas and views expressed in these pages are not borrowed from some company. They're all mine. These steps have been formulated and tested throughout my personal life and professional career. I've eliminated the high level "corporate speak" and replaced it with straightforward fresh talk that drives fresh results.

I purposely wrote this book because fresh is about now, it's about making it happen now. For too long, your customers have had to put up with your old, stale customer service and a-less-than-perfect customer experience—and don't deny it, your customer experience can be better. A lot better. Just ask your customers and see what they say.

You've kept your customers waiting way too long for Fresh Customer Service. Come along and enjoy the *fresh* journey!

Michael D. Brown, MBA

Introduction

"Research shows that your most satisfied customers go out of their way to actively try to convince others to do business with you. Unfortunately, dissatisfied customers make it a point to tell others to stay away, and dissatisfied customers are significantly more vocal…"

—J.D. Power and Associates

I'll make this quick. I know you're busy. We all know, and now a poll from the Associated Press reconfirms that, America is an impatient nation. We're a nation that gets antsy after five minutes on hold on the phone and fifteen minutes standing in a line. Almost one in four people in a May 2006 AP-Ipsos poll picked the grocery checkout as the line where their patience is mostly likely to melt like the ice cream in their cart. In short, we Americans want it all, and we want it NOW.

What greater proof do you need to realize that today's customers want **Fresh Customer Service** that exceeds their expectations? Your commitment to reading this book and implementing my ideas about delivering Fresh Customer Service will lead to a **World-Class customer service experience** that will, in turn, enhance the bottom line.

Humankind first encountered customer service back when our cave-dwelling ancestors bartered animal pelts for primitive wheels. OK, this is just a hunch, but I know the trials and travails of keeping customers smiling and coming back has been an arduous task for those who need to make a profit to prosper, which basically means everyone. The origin of the modern concept of customer service can actually be traced back to the craftsman economy of the 1800s, when individuals and small groups of manufacturers competed to produce arts and crafts that met the public demand.

I can't tell you if that era's customer service was good or bad. But what I can tell you with complete assurance is that companies are still struggling to deliver an effective customer service experience today—one that keeps customers satisfied, returning, and spreading the gospel of that company's services and products—and that many companies have made a strong commitment to customer service, which is critically important to the company's bottom line.

Yet often the "customer service commitment" is delivered via ill-defined, stale programs. Short-term initiatives are force-fed to apprehensive employees through glossy print materials with vague, inadequate phrases such as "Customers Are #1," "Treat Every Customer Right," and "Take Care of the Customer." Employees forget about these lame, clichéd slogans as soon as they have read them, just like you already have.

Year after year, after they've racked their brains for catchy phrases, upselling, cross-selling, and any other customer service gimmick you can name, leaders and managers bump their heads against the wall and stand in disbelief that their customer service performance is stagnant or, worse yet, declining.

The current norm is to downsize training and reduce funds spent on developing employees and making a great experience for the customer. Reward and Recognition (R&R) is down and investment in the employees typically amounts to peanuts. Most of the aforementioned customer service strategies are outdated. Few actually work. Don't forget: You get what you pay for. And often customers get much less than that—and they know it.

In this age, a customer can find your services duplicated or your products cheaper on the next block. The one way you can differentiate yourself in a sea of similar competition is by offering exemplary customer service. This will never happen if you use the same stale, outdated, failed approach to customer service that you and your competitors have always used before.

The business world needs a makeover. A new perspective. A fresh approach. Fresh Customer Service demystifies the process of attracting loyal, happy customers who return again and again and recommend your business to their friends and families. This type of customer reaction, what some may consider as a minor detail, can actually tip the scales and prove the difference between a prosperous organization and a bankrupt organization. So what's the secret? *The Frontline Employee.*

This secret is actually more of an idea, one that started to blossom in me as a child growing up in poverty-stricken Mississippi. The idea set root in my psyche as I became a hardworking Frontline Employee in the beginning of my professional career, and is now the reason for my success. This idea is the key to unlocking sustained long-term success in whatever area of service or production your organization offers. Throughout your organization's entire process of selling, serving, marketing, cleaning—you name it—the only way you can hope to deliver a World-Class customer service experience is by listening to, involving, and valuing the feedback and expertise your Frontline Employees can offer.

What? What did I just hear? Was that you lamenting that customer service is just one more thing to worry about—a thorn in your side that is being twisted and pushed deeper by the unpredictable market and pressure from shareholders that seems to rise by the hour? I know, I know, the struggle to turn just-any-old customer into a loyal customer is un-yielding, and the burden of competition is so stiff you don't have time to think about what Mary Jo at the cash register and Frank the Janitor have to say about things.

But these are the exact people to whom you need to lis-ten and show your appreciation—the operator who answers customer complaint calls, the construction worker who is building a new home, the consultant who is trying to move a client, the greeter who welcomes the customer at the en-trance of the store, the cashier who tallies the customer's total at the register. The associate on the floor who explains why this appliance is better than that one, who offers to help carry grocery bags, who tidies up the restrooms, who smiles when he performs his duties, or anyone who comes in contact with the customer be it in person or via email, voice mail, snail mail, Instant Message, Live Chat, or what-ever Internet-based form of communication has sprouted up this week.

If you are a manager, frontline leader, supervisor, entrepre-neur, director, HR rep, small business owner, or CEO and you can offer your Frontline Employees a healthy, fruitful, cohesive working environment where their contributions are valued and respected, the Frontline Employees will take care of the customers. And the customers will be loyal customers, and the bottom line will reflect it.

Remember this important business fact:
The employee is number one, not the customer.
The customer is number two.

As I mentioned in the preface, this is a radical notion that flies in the face of everything you have ever learned about customer service. But if the common wisdom regarding customer service is right, why is there an almost universal agreement among the shopping public that customer service stinks? Allow me to repeat this near-heresy of customer service philosophy: The employee is number one, not the customer. The customer is number two.

The key to running a successful operation is to believe and to practice the concept that customers should always come second—employees matter more in the immediate sense and should therefore come first. After all, happy employees unleash their enthusiasm and passion from within, and that passion is contagious. It infects everyone around them, including customers.

Frontline Employees need to genuinely feel appreciated, motivated, and important. If you ever hope to provide a

World-Class customer service experience through the 6.5 steps of Fresh Customer Service, then you need to take care of the Frontline Employee first. Passionate and motivated employees deliver a World-Class customer service experience quicker, better, and more consistently.

Several years ago, I worked for a company in Little Rock, Arkansas. The business I managed was experiencing 250 percent employee turnover, lagging sales, and an apathetic frontline team. Many of the employees were only temporary because the business had a difficult time retaining people.

After I had been working there about thirty days, my manager came to me and said, "You know, the leadership team has commented that the operation runs completely differently when you're in charge. And I can also see that our sales numbers are 15 to 20 percent higher when you're leading the team." He went on to ask, "How do you keep employees motivated and coming back to work every day?" At the time, the temporary employees would work a couple of days and not return.

I thought about it and replied, "I guess it's the way I treat them." To be honest, I didn't know then why the employees were eager to work for me or why my numbers were so high. About six months after I left that company, I got a call from one of the Frontline Employees still working there. Her name was Gladys.

"The other employees and I just wanted to call and say hello," Gladys said. I was delighted to hear from her, and from the rest of my former employees through her. Gladys continued, "Michael, it's not the same since you left, and everybody misses you. We really liked working with you." I asked Gladys, "What's so different?"

"Michael, the manager asked me the other day to polish the brass railing," Gladys said. "He must be crazy to think that I'm going to get on my hands and knees to polish the brass railing. I'm not doing that. It's not my job."

I was shocked to hear Gladys make that comment. After all, she had been a very loyal employee when I was there. I said to Gladys, "What's the big deal with polishing the brass? You did it when I was there."

"Michael," she replied, "it's the way you asked us to do things, and the way you treated us. You always said 'thank you' even if we did something that was our job. We always wanted to do our very best for you."

I truly believe customer service is improved when we put Frontline Employees like Gladys first. I delivered this message to about twenty-five frontline managers in Van Nuys, California. In my talk, I related my idea about how I consider customers to be not number one, but number two. If we take care of the Frontline Employees, I said, and treat them as if they are our number-one priority, they will in turn take care of our customers. Once the customers are taken care of politely, efficiently, and in a timely manner, they will continue to seek our company's business and refer us to their friends and family. That's when the money comes in.

And happy employees naturally provide superior customer service. They smile. I've learned ways to make employees happy, and one simple way is by thanking them every day. Thank them for going above and beyond their job descriptions—look how it made Gladys feel. And why not thank them for doing what they're supposed to be doing? It sure can't hurt anyone.

When I said this, the managers started clapping. In fact, my manager, Stephanie, later confided in me: "When you said that the employees are number one, I wanted to come up and shake your hand."

A few days later, I ran into Bernard, another manager who had attended my presentation. He told me he had subsequently held a meeting with his staff and told them all he cared about them and thanked them for doing an outstanding job during the previous month. He said his employees smiled at him in shock. The shock must have been from actually hearing him say something nice for once!

The Frontline Employee is the most important asset, resource, and ally to an organization's operations. He and his quest to deliver a World-Class customer service experience are paramount. We must take care of all of our Frontline Employees first if we ever hope to effectively and consistently reach the customer. We must treat each employee with the utmost trust, honesty, respect, integrity, and commitment to his or her well-being.

We should always seek to maximize the talent of each employee and work to enhance his or her quality of life. We must also value diversity among our staff and work to fulfill their personal aspirations. Only then will the Frontline Employee be more apt to pour his or her heart into providing a World-Class customer service experience and delivering the goals and objectives of the organization.

Empower the Frontline Employees

In order to inspire pride, excitement, teamwork, and fulfillment in the workplace, all employees should have the right to be involved in the planning of the work affecting them. In addition to providing a World-Class customer service experience to the customers, you want to ensure that the Frontline Employee is an ambassador for the organization.

The company's objectives, goals, aspirations, and expected customer experience should be communicated to all employees.

It is everyone's responsibility to support the empowerment of the Frontline Employees. When the customer has a problem or bad experience, the employee should have the tools and ability to Make-it-Right Now, which I cover in more depth in Fresh Step 3. Help the Frontline Employee make the customer's problems his problems. The instant satisfaction of the customer is the responsibility of every employee.

Let Frontline Employees know the priorities

The company's priorities and values need to be crystal clear in the minds of all Frontline Employees. Forcing them to work in ambiguous, uncertain "gray areas" of operation is like asking someone to walk a tightrope while blindfolded. It is simply a recipe for disaster. Whenever I take over a new team, I always establish a general theme or mission/priority statement. Here's one I have used before:

OUR TEAM
Always Exceeds Expectations!
"Safely deliver a World-Class customer service
experience that develops people, drives
performance, and protects the company's assets!"

For many individuals, organizations, corporations, mom-and-pop stores, and entrepreneurs, delivering a World-Class customer service experience through Fresh Customer Service will require a cultural change. But embracing this experience, no matter how much work it will take you, will deliver a competitive edge unlike any other. Our customers are asking—no, begging—for Fresh Customer Service, and if we provide it, we will be able to deliver a World-Class customer service experience *every time*. Serve the customer and beat the competition.... No company is successful, financially or otherwise, without Fresh Customer Service.

So, what are the concrete results of Fresh Customer Service?

While you're reading, keep in mind that if you can implement Fresh Customer Service, you will see remarkable results. You'll be able to align corporate strategies to better incorporate the core mission of customer service, and ultimately enhance the bottom line. You'll see an improved frontline execution of corporate strategies without sacrificing the customer experience. You'll be able to create awareness, empowerment, and tools that can be utilized by the Frontline Employees to **Make-It-Right Now** when customer problems or opportunities surface.

Furthermore, you'll see an increased confidence in frontline staff for the resolution of customer issues and increased consistency in response. You'll have a competitive, grounded customer service program as a part of the core business model. And finally, you'll be able to boast a high-speed response to the market that will help sustain a competitive advantage, as opposed to responding in a reactive way that will place your business in an inferior competitive position. Start putting these Fresh Steps into action and your bottom line will zoom upward.

About this Fresh Little Green Book...

My goal in writing this book was to offer you an informative, yet fun and easy, read that will help you deliver a World-Class customer service experience through Fresh Customer Service and get results. I can't count how many business and self-help books have piled up on my desk over the years, and how few I've actually read and enjoyed and were worth my time. This Fresh Little Green Book is a handy size that can be read on the go. Each chapter opens up with a Fresh appetizer to whet your appetite for more, and each chapter ends with charming cartoons sure to arouse a chuckle or two.

Throughout the book, you will find real life "fresh stories" that I have personally experienced. I have changed the names of many companies to protect those who don't know that they are providing something much less than a Fresh Customer Service experience.

I am confident that after leaders, managers, and Frontline Employees have read this book, I will experience Fresh Customer Service and a World-Class Customer service experience the next time I visit their organization, firm, or corporation. I am sure their Frontline Employees will be able to tell a much different story, as well.

One of my main hopes and aspirations is that this book will provide individuals, organizations, firms, and corporations with the awareness, tools, and support that will allow them to deliver Fresh Customer Service that delivers a World-Class experience. So that you don't have to just take my word, this book will also feature some News Fresh stories and research that will affirm the need for Fresh Customer Service, investment in the frontline and the importance of delivering a World-Class customer service experience.

This book will take you on a 6.5 Fresh Step journey of the Fresh Customer Service experience. Each step is presented in an approach I like to think of as a "Fresh Menu." Imagine creating a World-Class customer experience as being similar to baking a cake. No matter how clever you are in the kitchen, if you try to bake a cake with bad flour, it won't come out well. Similarly, bad Frontline ingredients will equal a bad customer experience.

Therefore, each full Fresh Step is broken out into a Fresh Appetizer, which is an assessment and benchmark of common customer service problems organizations face; a Fresh Entrée, which is the "main course" of action organizations should take to solve these problems; and a Temperature Check, which is a checklist to follow and see if your results are well-done and ready to serve, or are still rare and need a little more preparation before your customers are ready to consume them.

There is also a "Fresh Technologies" section to let all you technophiles (or even all you technophobes) out there know about some of the cutting-edge technological systems that can greatly aid your Fresh Customer Service efforts. Also sprinkled throughout are Fresh Bits, small nuggets of information to help you better implement the fresh step. Every Fresh Step ends with a Take Out section that quickly summarizes the three key points to keep in mind when performing that step.

You'll learn what Fresh Customer Service means, how to spot it (or the lack thereof) in your everyday experiences, how to implement it in your company, and how to instill it in your work team. By the time you've read through these quick, easy, fun Fresh Steps, you'll be ready to make the plunge and never go back to yesterday's old, stale, incompetent customer service.

So, What exactly is Fresh Customer Service? It's Fresh Understanding...

In the first Fresh Step, **Side-By-Side Walking**, I will teach you to how "walk a mile" in your Frontline Employees' shoes, to view their work from their perspective, to understand what they do and why they do it. Side-By-Side Walking will help give you a real-world understanding of the environment your Frontline Employees operate in, and separate perceptions from actual activities and true problems. Side-By-Side Walking is the foundation for understanding where your organization is at the moment, the gaps that exist, what is working and what needs improvement.

When you perform Side-By-Side Walking early in the process, you are able to make assessments and implement improvements that are grounded, executable, and relevant to the frontline. This leads to a more accelerated level of change and execution of your winning solutions to your customer service problem. Side-by-Side Walking provides you with a real view and helps you separate fact from fiction.

In Fresh Step 2, you'll learn how **Smart Tasking** clearly defines the critical tasks/processes that support the customer service offering and the deadlines by which they must be completed. The most important factor is completing the necessary tasks/processes without impeding the delivery of a World-Class customer service experience to the customer. Smart Tasking creates a harmonized balance between completing the tasks/processes and delivering a World-Class customer service experience.

It's Fresh Empowerment...

Make-It-Right Power, Fresh Step 3, instills both the responsibility and the authority to resolve customer complaints and issues in the Frontline Employees who are most able to satisfy the customer at any point in time. I'll tell you how I visited a leading furniture retailer, expecting top service and an advertised sale, but was greeted with a misleading sales promotion and a confused, powerless staff devoid of Make-It-Right Power.

In Fresh Step 4, I describe the **What-If Arsenal** employees in such situations need in order to do their jobs in a manner that promotes the World-Class customer experience. The What-If Arsenal builds on organizational experiences, reduces the need to reinvent the wheel while creating a fresh depository for Frontline Employees to make fresh deposits of "what-if solutions," and helps give Make-It-Right Power to the Frontline Employee to instantly serve and satisfy the customer.

It's Fresh Thinking...

Bubble-Up Innovation, the fifth Fresh Step, will show you how to appreciate and utilize the current ideas Frontline Employees possess to improve the whole organization. After all, Frontline Employees represent the face of the company. They come in contact with customers every day, day-in and day-out. They, not managers or CEOs, are privy to why senior customers want earlier store hours, or why the trash that accumulates on the sidewalk is keeping customers away. Therefore it is a winning practice to listen to the suggestions Frontline Employees may have to make your organization better.

Fresh Step 6, **Relentless Focus**, is the continual and consistent emphasis on the the Frontline Employee delivering a World-Class customer service experience and embedding this into the core business model, as opposed to customer service "programs-of-the-month."

Fresh Customer Service cannot be delegated to only one program a month, one part of the store, one level in the organization, one business function, or even just the customer service department. Fresh Customer Service, like a store-wide initiative that extends to the street corner and parking lot, is an ongoing process. It must be embodied in each and every worker every minute of the day and in all areas of sales, production, marketing, management, ownership, and customer service.

Finally, there is Fresh Step 6.5. That's right, you're not quite finished until you can **Make it Happen Now!** It's up to you to take it from there.

Something else you need to know about this book

Why is this book green? To me, the color green represents growth, results, money, life, relaxation, novelty, fertility, well-being, balance and order, learning, harmony, energy, freedom… and go! Green is good for the environment, especially when it comes to customers, Frontline Employees, and the creation of a World-Class customer experience.

So here are instructions on how to read this book. Whether you are an executive, a frontline leader, a supervisor, a Frontline Employee, or even a customer, this book is for you! Whether you are an entrepreneur launching your own business, on the career path at an established firm, or a dedicated employee of a non-profit organization, you can apply the 6.5 Fresh Steps to provide Fresh Customer Service to the people who keep you in business.

And you can read and interpret this book via several Fresh methods.

Go to the website (**www.themichaeldbrown.com**) and stare at the Fresh Customer Service Artwork and form your own interpretation of the Fresh Step. And if you are not a strictly visual learner, then simply turn the pages and begin to read the fresh text. If at the end of reading the fresh text you feel like you need help in benchmarking your Fresh Customer Service activities, then read the Temperature Check. If you're really in a hurry, or maybe would just like a little reinforcement of what you are learning, Take Out summarizes the three most important aspects of each Fresh Step.

Now if you have become a bit gloomy (because you realize that you, your business, organization, firm, or group is nowhere near delivering a World-Class customer service experience through the Frontline Employee) then read the Fresh Last Words cartoons at the end of each chapter and pick up a chuckle or two. The Fresh Last Words cartoons are a dialogue, spat, argument, or disagreement that occurs between Ms. Old Penny and Mr. Fresh Green Back. Log on to my website at **www.themichaeldbrown.com** and tell me who you think is right.

Now relax and enjoy the freshness!

For more information on other material and products that accompany this book, please visit
www.themichaeldbrown.com

Fresh Step ❶
Side-By-Side Walking

 **Fresh Appetizer:**
The Chips 'n' Sips Story

At a certain fast-paced retail chain—I'll protect its real identity and call it "Chips 'n' Sips"—declining sales were the source of sleepless nights, headaches, and heated arguments among the increasingly frustrated leadership team. The company's marketing experts finally put their heads together and decided to implement a new cross-selling program that they introduced to all the employees with great fanfare.

The program used colorful, attention-grabbing printed marketing materials. To help cashiers with their new cross-selling task, managers provided a set of bookmark-sized laminated "cheat cards" with several items to suggest.

These cards were placed at all Chips 'n' Sips registers to remind the cashiers what items to cross-sell with each purchase. If a customer bought milk, the cashier was to offer her bread (the laminated cards showed a picture of a milk carton with an arrow pointing to a loaf of bread). If another customer bought beer, the cashier was to suggest chips (same picture format). The cashiers started to follow this procedure but soon became discouraged by the number of rejections they were experiencing.

The bread being cross-sold with the milk was located several feet away from the checkout stand, likewise for the chips being cross-sold with the beer. Customers were reluctant to give up their spots in line to go and pick up the suggested items—we all know how more than a few minutes in line are unacceptable to today's shopper. The handful of customers who decided to get out of line and return with a cross-sold item were greeted by the other customers' looks of hatred and disgust for holding up the line.

In short, this cross-selling program was a disaster. It held up the lines and de-motivated the cashiers because of non-stop rejections. Had the marketers and senior managers been more in touch with the layout of the stores, the way cashiers operated, and customers' shopping styles, they would have understood this promotional method was doomed from the get-go. This futile attempt at boosting sales ended up costing Chips 'n' Sips more than $100,000.

I knew there had to be a better way to do this, so when Chips 'n' Sips hired me to help grow their business and the efficiency and effectiveness of their Frontline Employees, one of my first contributions to the business was offering a cross-selling process based on a completely different strategy. Before I offered any ideas, I went to a local Chips 'n' Sips outlet and took note of how registers were set up, where products were located in the store, and what cashiers had to do during the failed cross-selling program.

This insider's look at the business helped me develop a plan. I began by asking a Chips 'n' Sips store manager to select a special item to promote each day. Every morning, that day's item was placed in a basket next to the register, and the cashiers simply had to cross-sell the item located at arm's length to the checkout stand. That way, customers could continue checking out without having to get out of line.

After following this process for three weeks, we began to ask Frontline Employees to select an item. You can only imagine how fast the items that the Frontline Employees selected sold. You guessed right, it was easy for them to sell a product that they liked and believed in. The cashiers received fifty-four percent fewer rejections.

Side-By-Side Walking, which I like to describe as walking a mile in the shoes of employees to understand what they do, how they do it, and how they experience their jobs, would have helped the Chips 'n' Sips leadership team tremendously. It didn't take me much time to visit a store and see for myself that the less-than-stellar cross-selling program was self-destructing right before my eyes.

If the marketing managers themselves had taken the time to go out and see how difficult it was for cashiers to cross-sell a product, only to make a customer wait in line longer and be the recipient of scowls from other customers, they never would have implemented their cross-selling program. Side-By-Side Walking would have prevented the original difficulties with the cross-selling program because the marketing department would have understood the importance of customer flow and the negative impact constant rejections would have on Frontline Employee morale.

Why is Side-By-Side Walking Important?
Developing a program in conjunction with employees is better than developing a program for them without their input. A program with many points-of-view behind it will inevitably be better received and implemented. Side-By-Side Walking also helps managers and other non-Frontline Employees consider and appreciate the Frontline Employees' entire range of tasks and spectrums of experience. Side-By-Side Walking equips the non-Frontline Employee with

a fresh viewpoint and frontline perspective that should be incorporated into all decisions, programs, and strategies that are to be executed at the frontline and/or will impact the frontline.

To truly maximize the value you get from your Side-By-Side Walking experience, prepare for it with an unannounced, undercover site visit where you pose as a customer. Pick a store, warehouse, office, plant, or any other location where Frontline Employees are present, but where none of the employees or customers will recognize you, so that you are treated the same as all the other customers and go through an identical experience. By bringing the customer viewpoint into your Side-By-Side Walking effort, you will obtain a truly panoramic view of the frontline environment and may obtain some insights you would otherwise miss.

There are other "mystery methods" that will also work, depending on your type of business. For example, send an email to the company or organization complaining of a common problem and experience the method/process through which they provide (or fail to provide) resolution. You can do the same via a phone call, snail mail, or the ever-popular live chat. If you want to get an even more astonishing surprise, use one of the above methods during off-peak times, such as late hours, weekends, and holidays.

Fresh Entrée:
The 10 Steps of Side-by-Side Walking

Step 1. Make safety a priority. Prior to engaging in Side-By-Side Walking, the manager (or other non-frontline personnel) placing himself in the employee's shoes should be familiar with the role's appropriate safety procedures and policies. It is, after all, the employee's responsibility to follow safety rules.

Focusing on enhancing the bottom line does your organization little good if you disregard your employees' safety at work. Safety, like Mother always said, should come first. The cost of performing work in an unsafe manner—i.e. you don't follow fire and first aid codes and something goes awry—can erase profits and wreak havoc on your organization's reputation.

For example, the safety rule for construction companies requires all employees to wear hard hats before entering a construction site. If you are in the position to enter a worksite, you should happily and enthusiastically apply the hard hat to your head—even if it ruffles your hair or makes your head look bigger. Failing to follow these necessary rules will not only set a bad example, but it can also impede a World-Class customer service experience.

Early in my management career, I dealt with a situation that taught me about the importance of putting safety first and the problems that can arise when safety is not properly accounted for. I held a management position with a national hotel chain I'll call Majestic Suites. I was assigned to a location in Arkansas. After being there for about five weeks, I asked an employee to lift a box. She lifted it, and the next thing I knew, she was saying, "I heard something crack," and then going on to tell me how she had a bad back and that her doctor had forbidden her to lift anything weighing more than five pounds.

There had been nothing in the employee training program about how to properly lift an object, and nobody had ever asked her if she had any medical conditions that would make it unsafe for her to lift objects. In addition, as a new manager, I didn't know what to do when one of my employees announced she had injured her back. For both of us, the focus of our training had been on making the company money and doing our jobs.

From that point forth, I'd take every new employee around and show them things like the proper way to lift, how to use a knife, and how to mop the floor. It was all about the employee staying safe in everything they did and knowing the hazards from day one. I also established standard procedures to respond to employee injuries when they did happen, and performed regular daily walk-throughs of the site to see if any new hazards had popped up.

As for that incident with the bad back, we had caused harm to an employee, which cost the company seven to eight years of workman's compensation claims, which was a huge financial blow. In addition to physically hurting the employee, the incident threw the whole customer experience off, since as manager I didn't know how to deal with an injured employee and was distracted from serving the customers.

Step 2. Describe the job in a written document outlining tasks, constraints, and desired outcomes. Before you start the actual Side-By-Side Walking experience, be sure to secure a copy of the formal job description for the job that you will be observing. After reading the job description, write down your interpretation of what you think the job is about and state what you believe are the tasks, constraints, and the desired outcomes.

To illustrate this point, a well-known gas station chain asked me to come in and speak to new Frontline Employees about their launch of a revolutionary style of retailing. My week-long seminar focused on how to provide a "best in class" customer service environment and become ambassadors of the company's brand.

I went through my spiel of providing great service and representing this new retail concept that gave consumers other ways of purchasing the product. After an hour and a half, I mentioned that part of promoting this new concept would be cleaning windows and restrooms. The whole mood of the room changed. Thirty motivated employees who were eager and excited to become brand ambassadors quickly changed into thirty disgruntled, dissatisfied employees who wanted nothing to do with this new program.

"How does cleaning the windows and restrooms tie into the job description we were given?" asked one employee.

Another said that due to a medical condition, she couldn't be outside for an extended period of time, especially in the cold. Other employees complained they hadn't been informed there was this level of physicality to the job, and further stated that had they known, they would have never applied for the job.

We started out with a group of thirty employees training to be brand ambassadors, but by the end of the week that number had dwindled to twenty-two. They didn't understand fully what they'd been expected to do, and the person who wrote the job description didn't understand how important it was for Frontline Employees to know all the expectations from the very beginning. Once an employee is on the job and thinking they've come to do one thing, when a manager starts piling additional tasks on them, they feel dumped on.

In every organization, there is a need to continually look at job descriptions and search for "scope creep." The job description you wrote five years ago may no longer be applicable. The only way to know for sure is to perform Side-By-Side Walking with your Frontline Employees. You can quickly develop a set of job requirements that is overwhelming, as the thought process often becomes, "if it's feasible to get from point A to point B, then we should go on to point C."

For example, a while back Starbucks had a down day on the stock market, which many investors saw as a sign that luxury goods customers were no longer spending money. This caused a ripple effect throughout the luxury goods sector, until Starbucks announced the real reason for the sudden dip in their stock price.

According to an Associated Press article, Starbucks executives "blamed the slide on unexpectedly high demand for Frappuccinos and other frozen blended beverages in the peak morning hours, when baristas generally crank out more hot espresso drinks." The article goes on to credit Starbucks Chief Executive Jim Donald with saying the company was "working to solve the problem by having more baristas work the morning peak hours, among other possible changes, including reducing the time it takes to blend cold drinks."

When you introduce a new product but keep the same employees and processes, you have to make sure you're not really killing your business. By validating and revalidating your job description versus your actual frontline experience, you will quickly get the message if you "missed the boat" with any of your plans.

I do have to offer much credit and kudos to Starbucks for owning up to their operational challenges and quickly putting solutions in place. I certainly think this is a step in the right direction and will likely prove to be a good solution.

Step 3. Prepare yourself mentally and understand the purpose of this process. Until you fully relinquish your former title, position of authority, and management attitude, you will not be able to wholeheartedly understand the Frontline Employees' job while you're walking in his shoes. In some instances, those who perform Side-By-Side Walking will be on their feet all day, only have short breaks, and come in contact with customers regularly. Every experience that you have will be a window into your Frontline Employees' lives at work and what they encounter on a daily basis.

In a multitasking world, I've worked with upper management types who say they want to walk side-by-side through their Frontline Employees' experience, but still bring their Blackberry along. They are going through the motions of Side-By-Side Walking rather than immersing themselves into their company's frontline experience. They never mentally check out of the office and into the frontline environment. You need to fully get into the same state of mind that your frontline employees are in. If you remain in your current management role, it will be much harder for you to understand the gaps that may or may not exist in your frontline environment.

Step 4. Adopt the physical accouterments of the Frontline Employee, such as dress, earplugs, goggles, nametags, hat, apron, etc. You must look and feel like the Frontline Employee, and the uniform is a large part of the overall experience. So try it on. Go to work wearing the uniform. Is it flattering? Is it made of quality material? Or is it downright ugly, itchy, or in other ways uncomfortable to wear? Be honest; is it a color even your grandmother would consider out of style? You'll experience firsthand why employees like or dislike their uniforms.

Knowing what it feels like to wear and work in the uniform will help you understand how, if needed, it could be improved. If there are any resulting subsequent changes, you'll notice less resistance from your staff about wearing the required garb.

Think about this for a second—would you be a happy employee if you didn't like what you were wearing, or would your discomfort/dislike somehow be expressed on your face and interfere with your providing a World-Class customer service experience? Think about how miserable you were the last time your collar was a bit too tight. Ladies, think about the last time you wore shoes that caused a pain so sharp you wanted to scream.

Now do you get the point of how uniforms/dress codes can either make for a good day or a miserable day? Take a minute and ask the Frontline Employees what they think of the uniforms; you might be surprised.

For example, I once worked with Frontline Employees at a strongly competitive retail chain in Atlanta, Georgia. Most of them had to take the bus to work. Their uniforms were these really archaic green/blue shirts with a huge logo on the left side of the chest. They all hated to wear the shirts and would usually come to work in their street clothes and then change into their uniforms.

"Why don't you just wear your uniforms to work?" I asked them.

"Because the uniforms are hideous," was the universal reply. The employees were primarily from a younger population and were embarrassed by the uniforms they were forced to wear. Management had not changed the style of the uniforms in eight years. My recommendation was to go with a sportier, polo-type shirt with a smaller logo and looser collar. Management listened, and changed their uniforms to look more like regular polo shirts with smaller logos, not to mention be made of more breathable cotton fabric!

Employees started wearing their uniforms to work, and came in each day in a good mood and a sense of pride in how they looked. Now I am not saying that if you just provide the Frontline Employees with hip and chic uniforms, they will instantly be happy and deliver a World-Class customer service experience. Instead, I am saying this is a critical and important steppingstone in the process of putting employees first and valuing them.

Even more importantly, the time being lost to employees changing when they arrived was no longer an issue. The people who made the purchase decisions on corporate uniforms had never before tried them on or gotten any input from the Frontline Employees who had to live in them during the work day.

Also, when you come in and look like them, Frontline Employees make the connection that, "if the uniform is good enough for the senior managers, it's good enough for me." Furthermore, employees and customers won't be as open and revealing to you if you're in a suit. Employees will give you exactly the kind of experience they think you want, instead of revealing problems to you.

Step 5. Complete all the pre-work steps of the Frontline Employee such as clocking in, preparing the cash register and shift routine sheet, reviewing the new guest roster to gauge the workload, reviewing sales targets and goals for the shift, setting up the call center with today's documents, and reading the task board. It is important to complete all the pre-work steps, processes, and procedures required of the Frontline Employee. If you are going to do this, you may as well do it thoroughly to get the most out of the experience.

A senior manager for the same retail chain that successfully upgraded its uniforms asked me to take him through the "gut" of the operation, starting with initial Frontline Employee-customer contact. He didn't understand that there was a whole process before the employee ever dealt with the customer. In a case like this, it's easy for a manager to say, "This is all they have to do? They should also be doing X, Y, and Z."

When the preparation doesn't go well, a Frontline Employee can be set up for an entire shift that doesn't go well, which parlays to a customer experience that is lacking and a bottom line that suffers. The senior manager who wanted to get the nuts and bolts of his store's frontline experience didn't realize that there is a whole separate process before the experience even starts.

Step 6. Follow the processes that are currently in place. Be careful not to try to influence the protocol or be judgmental. Instead of viewing Side-By-Side Walking as just another exercise you have to get through before you can go back to your nice comfortable office, you must convince yourself that the Frontline Employee's position is now the job you have day-in and day-out. Otherwise, you will never get all the information you can about the Frontline Employee's job or the firsthand challenges this individual faces in providing a World-Class customer service experience.

If you go in with the mentality of just going through the motions, you will finish with a false perspective, diminishing the work and the role of the Frontline Employee. Don't let this happen. And don't forget, customers will see that you aren't engaged and that your job isn't something worth committing to. Remember, you are now the face to the customer and responsible for delivering Fresh Customer Service, which leads to a World-Class customer service experience.

The same retail chain senior manager who asked me to show him the operational "gut" immediately began to attack the processes in place as soon as he walked into the store site. His criticisms were mostly in favor of the employees. But his critiques produced more of a distraction than any positive result. Now the employees had a sense he didn't like the way things worked, and they were prejudiced to only show him things they thought he would like, so as not to get the shift manager in trouble.

They took on a "we won't let him see this" mentality. This made it extremely difficult to evaluate the whole process at the end and determine what was missing (there were other factors that made evaluating the frontline environment in this particular instance difficult, but we'll get to those short-ly!). You should wait untill the end of the day to perform a full evaluation and see what's preventing your organiza-tion from offering a World-Class customer experience, as opposed to critiquing as you go while in the presence of Frontline Employees and customers.

Step 7. Observe the individual processes and tasks that occur during the shift. Observing the Frontline Employ-ees' duties is one of the most critical components of Side-By-Side Walking. You'll want to watch everything about the operation, such as when, how, and how often things are done, as well as the tools that are used to carry out each task. After you have a good idea about how systems work, then you'll want to ask particular questions about the protocol so that you know exactly what's going on at every moment of a typical shift. You also want to be observant of how task ex-ecution adds to or subtracts from the customer experience.

The same senior manager was too preoccupied with find-ing flaws as he went along to carefully observe individual processes. When you're preoccupied, you're not there men-tally, and there are some processes employees perform that are seamless which you'll never catch unless you say, "I'd like to see everything you're doing and not take anything for granted."

Step 8. Complete the entire shift, from the pre-shift work through the closing process. You've made it this far; cutting corners here will only hurt you in the long run. Sticking around for the full shift can be a lot to ask of a busy executive, manager, or other stakeholder, but there are processes that only happen at the end of shift, and if you miss them, you won't get the entire experience, meaning you can't make informed decisions.

Our friend the senior manager shortchanged his experience by leaving halfway through the process. Believe it or not, he thought he had a clear understanding of the frontline experience. He went back to his office proud that he now had a grasp on a very critical part of the business.

What he didn't realize was that he didn't get to experience the peak time of the business, the afternoon. This was also the time where he would have seen what employees stated as their greatest challenge: Processing credit cards when there were several customers using a credit card at the same time. Once several credit cards were swiped one right after another, the network would slow to a crawl. Customers would become physically and mentally frustrated with the length of time it was taking for the card to process, which would cause undue stress on the employee.

Step 9. Reflect on the experience and compare it with the formal job description. Look for differences and gaps between the actual job description and what tasks are being completed. This is also a good time to align the Side-By-Side Walking experience with the stated policies and procedures. Ask yourself this question: Do the policies and procedures that are in place help or hinder the customer service process, and do they enhance or inhibit the customer experience?

Don't confuse a site visit with Side-By-Side Walking. A site visit often lasts thirty minutes to an hour and allows only a brief glimpse of employee activity. Side-By-Side Walking is about immersing yourself in the Frontline Employee's experience from beginning to end. Anything less than full immersion shortchanges the full Side-By Side Walking experience and leaves you with a foggy understanding of the role of the Frontline Employee. Be prepared to do Side-By-Side Walking from beginning to end.

Step 9 is one of the most critical steps. Get a realistic expectation of the experience. How is it delivered? Does anything hinder, hamper or enhance the customer experience?

If you walk away saying, "This isn't what we intended," or "The way we intended doesn't work," go back and look for the gaps between what you want and what you're getting. Do they appear from the onset of operations, or do they pop up later on in the day? How do you hold people accountable? How do you fill the gaps once you discover them—more training, creating a more competitive environment, etc.? In the case of the manager who left at lunch, he thought the company could do more on the frontline with fewer resources. He only saw the initial morning peak, followed by a two-hour lull. Based on the lull, he advocated that Frontline Employees do more with reduced staffing numbers and hours. Fortunately, his suggestions weren't implemented.

Step 10. And finally, describe any possible improvements in a written document. This form should then be shared with the rest of the leadership team. The stakeholders who are serious about delivering a World-Class customer experience should review the document and see how its insight can change and improve their established policies and the customer experience.

It would be great if you could share the gaps with the people who are responsible for crafting the job descriptions as well as with the leadership team who is responsible for setting expectations of the Frontline Employees and the customer experience. Don't forget to include your reflections from Step 9.

Also, don't be afraid to go beyond the job description in your process document. Track scope creep; track the customer side of the frontline experience. At any point is there something missing?

Remember that every employee in the company has a responsibility to provide a World-Class customer service experience—even those who aren't on the frontline. That means that if you are a CEO or manager, this applies to you, too. It's natural for people who work in the corporate office or in some offsite location to want to critique the way a process is executed when it's not them who has to do the executing.

But the purpose of Side-By-Side Walking is not to provide fodder for critique. The purpose is to gain a real frontline experience, so that this experience will weigh on all your further decisions.

After all, if you are a manager, leader, or CEO, you're likely seen as a person of authority; your opinions and critiques carry a significant amount of weight in the eyes of the Frontline Employees. Walking a mile in their shoes will show you what sitting in your comfortable office chair never could.

Finally, you should be an advocate for your organization's policies and procedures, even though you may disagree with them. And don't be surprised if employees want to use your Side-By-Side Walking exercise as an opportunity to tell you about how bad the policies and procedures are, how the pay is too low, and how the company is clueless.

You should listen but remain a neutral advocate and ambassador for the company, though afterwards you should share this feedback with the appropriate decision makers once you leave the location. Remember that the Frontline Employees are performing the task, process, or job day-in and day-out. They are intimate with their work, they know what is right and wrong for the customer, and they know what is needed to deliver a World-Class customer experience.

Just try asking them for their views, but be prepared to do one thing: shut up and listen. After you have fully listened, if you don't agree, be prepared to offer and explain the reason why, don't just revert to some company line such as, "I don't agree, end of story."

Temperature Check

Let your Frontline Employees help you answer these questions. Go ahead; don't be afraid to ask them for their input. They're surely nice enough people, they take care of the customers, and they make your mortgage payment possible.

1. Do I really understand what a typical day is like for the Frontline Employee?

2. Have I fully read the job description of the Frontline Employee?

3. Do the policies and procedures that we have in place actually enhance the customer experience?

4. Do the policies and procedures hinder my Frontline Employees from delivering a World-Class customer service experience to our customers?

5. Do I really know and understand the impact that my decisions and my job have on the Frontline Employee and the customer experience?

6. By Side-By-Side Walking for a day with Frontline Employees, will I lose some of my power and authority or will this experience do the opposite to my image?

6.5 Is Side-By-Side Walking with the Frontline Employees a great time for me to tell them what we at the home office think they can do to better perform a job?

If you can honestly answer "yes" to Questions 1, 2, 3, 5, and 6.5, "no" to Question 4, and in response to Question 6 say that your image will be enhanced among Frontline Employees, your Side-By-Side Walking effort is well-done and the results are ready to serve to the entire organization.

The temperature chart on the following page will help illustrate how close you are to having prepared a complete Side-By-Side Walking entrée. Count the total number of "correct" answers you gave based on the guidelines in the preceding paragraph, and then check your correct response rate. You will discover how your entrée is currently cooked (rare, medium rare, medium, medium well or well done), and you can also consult a brief explanation of what this means for your organization. If you have some answers that don't match up, you probably need to get back in the kitchen and do a little more cooking!

What's your Temperature? Side-By-Side Walking

Temperature	Correct Response Rate	Explanation
Rare	0 correct Temperature Check responses	Your executives have never interacted with any Frontline Employees and probably have barely ventured within the Frontline environment!
Medium Rare	1-2 correct Temperature Check responses	Executives have performed site visits and maybe done some perfunctory Fontline Employee interviews, but not much more.
Medium	3-4 correct Temperature Check responses	Executives have spent some time in the Frontline Employee's shoes, but how much of the information gained has been brought back to the boardroom/decision table?
Medium Well	5-6 correct Temperature Check responses	Executives have performed a full Side-By-Side Walking exercise and documented the experience. Now it's time for a little soul-searching based on the results.
Well Done	6.5 correct Temperature Check responses	Executives have performed a full Side-By-Side Walking exercise, documented the results, and applied what they have learned to ensure that frontline policies and procedures benefit both employees and customers. This effort has enhanced executives' standing on the frontline.

*Keep checking the temperature to make sure you get to Well Done and stay there

News Fresh

According to Chris Denove and James D. Power IV of J.D. Power and Associates in their book, *Satisfaction: How Every Great Company Listens to the Voice of the Customer,* loyalty is only one of the ways that customer satisfaction drives profits. Their research shows that consumers will pay a hefty price premium to do business with a company that has a reputation for delivering steady high levels of customer satisfaction. This even holds true where the choices offered by competitors are generally the same.

Not only will satisfied customers pay more to do business with you, they will return to do business with you on a regular basis. This is a very important factor, because in most industries, consumers spread their business across multiple companies.

Furthermore, the *Wall Street Journal* reports that even the major airlines are realizing that a splurge in customer service will work wonders for the bottom line. Reporter Scott McCartney cites one example with Delta Airlines: "Delta put flight attendants in new uniforms last year hoping to improve morale. Indeed, the company found that after donning the new uniforms flight attendants treated customers better. Customer complaints dropped by half." Jim Whitehurst, Delta's chief operating officer, said that "having better morale among employees really helps the operation."

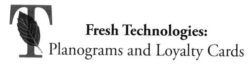

Fresh Technologies:
Planograms and Loyalty Cards

In the case of Chips 'n' Sips, automated planogramming systems could provide a useful tool to scientifically redesign store layout, product placement, and customer flow to maximize sales and customer convenience. Planogramming software employs sophisticated algorithms and formulas to determine how a particular retailer can best design its shopping environment, based on the wants and needs of its customer demographic.

Any retailer seeking to improve profits through cross-selling or upselling would be wise to enact a loyalty program. Using data mining technology, retailers can track the individual shopping behavior of loyalty program participants, who generally announce their presence by swiping a loyalty card at checkout. Advanced data mining systems can instantly recommend cross-sell and upsell opportunities based on that particular customer's purchase history, and transmit that data to the point-of-sale terminal via Internet connection. The retailer can then print out a special coupon for the customer at the point-of-sale, which can be redeemed at that time or during a future purchase.

Fresh Bit

Do you want a handy checklist to get you started with your Side-By-Side Walking exercise? Go to www.themichaeld-brown.com, register by clicking on the mdb network if you are a first time user, and go to the Fresh Customer Service Section and select Side-By-Side Walking.

Take Out

1. Side-By-Side Walking is the foundation of the 6.5 Fresh Steps your organization must follow to achieve Fresh Customer Service. It is the only way to obtain a true assessment of the strengths and weaknesses of your Frontline Employees, and of the validity and effectiveness of the daily processes and procedures they must follow to do their jobs and to truly understand what kind of customer experience has been delivered and identify gaps and opportunities between what has actually been delivered vs. the intended customer experience. Without an initial Side-By-Side Walking exercise, effective implementation of Fresh Customer Service will be impossible.

2. Side-By-Side Walking is only effective if you fully commit to the entire process. This means carrying out each of the ten steps in its entirety, from making safety a priority to describing the job in a written document to completing an entire shift in full uniform to reflecting upon and documenting your experience. There are no short-cuts, and there is no way to skip or streamline a step without substantially reducing the value your Side-By-Walking exercise will provide.

3. Side-By-Side Walking will only provide lasting value with an organizational commitment to follow-up. After a walk is completed, senior management must carefully review the data collected to determine how to best improve the frontline experience, and Frontline Employees must actively provide ideas and feedback both during and after the walk. Executives and managers must be willing to undergo Side-By-Walking exercises on a regular basis, and Frontline Employees must be willing to make those exercises as informative as possible. Managers and Frontline Employees need to create an atmosphere of mutual respect and trust where ideas and observations can be freely exchanged.

Fresh Step ❷
Smart Tasking

Fresh Appetizer:
Confessions of a Caffeine Junkie

On a hot day in July, I drove up to a Rancho Cucamonga, California branch of one of the most popular coffee shops in the state, to get the day's dose of my favorite coffee concoction on ice. I ordered the light version, of course, because it's minus the calories (yet I just can't seem to resist re-loading it with milk, white sugar, cane sugar, and a pinch of Splenda).

Try navigating your way through California's congested streets and you'll notice you need more caffeine and sugar, too—not only to keep you alert of the guy who just cut you off for the fourth time, but also to help keep a smile on your face when the lady next to you decides to drive in both your lane and hers at the same time.

The store soon came into sight, and I noticed the first bad omen: a line was snaking out the front door and onto the sidewalk. I'd seen lines like this at rock concerts, but for coffee? Needless to say, I weighed the options of waiting in line with the other caffeine junkies versus avoiding the experience altogether and forgoing my daily fix (neither one a pretty picture).

I chose to wait in line. I convinced myself it would move at a reasonable pace—after all, there were four employees behind the counter.

After standing in line for about three minutes, I saw a barista jet out from behind the counter with a bottle of blue cleaning liquid in hand. She pardoned herself for stepping in front of customers in the long line and rushed to the front door. Had some virus been spotted on the doorknob? She sprayed the door down and wiped so briskly you might have thought it had been contaminated with Ebola. Certainly a few fingerprints couldn't have kept her from tending to her customers, right?

However, the cleaning didn't end there. She went over to the condiment bar and started wiping it down and organizing it, placing every last sugar packet, straw, and mixer in its happy little home. Meanwhile, the line was growing like the federal deficit, and I had now been waiting for more than ten minutes. My jaw dropped as I watched this extremely perky employee pull out a different rag and dust the back shelves displaying kitschy coffee shop merchandise. Evidently she had already had her coffee fix.

My heart racing and my temperature rising, I couldn't bear the thought of waiting another minute for my drug—I mean, my coffee. So I approached the employee and asked, "Don't you think it's more important to get this line moving right now than it is to clean?" There are times where I think I have the right to coach any Frontline Employee or manager in the world (I think I bestowed this right upon myself).

"We have to clean every hour," she replied with a dimple on her cheek and a twinkle in her eye. "You wouldn't want to come into a dirty store, right?"

"I think that at this very moment your customers are more concerned that they are waiting in this long line as opposed to seeing if the back of the merchandise display rack is free of dust," I countered. "Maybe you should work on reducing the line first and dusting later." I didn't want to be a grouch, but by now I just couldn't take it anymore!

Smart Tasking, or creating a set of clear expectations and priorities for the staff, would have dramatically improved this customer service cataclysm. Smart Tasking would have empowered this employee to both meet cleaning standards—after the rush had subsided—and provide a World-Class customer service experience—now.

The problem here was not that the barista was following her prescribed tasks—the problem was that she was following them at an inopportune time, namely when customers were undergoing a long wait to be served. The young worker's priorities were convoluted. She did not feel empowered to hold off on the cleaning, even though it was rush hour, nor did she understand the consequences her decision to clean rather than to serve had on the overall customer experience.

Customer service became the casualty of a clean shelf. This employee was either not told or did not fully grasp the company's priority (which hopefully was providing World-Class customer service), and consequently, she made her customers unnecessarily wait in a long line for their caffeine. Never a good idea.

It is vitally important for any organization, large or small, to prioritize the tasks the Frontline Employee is supposed to perform so that a World-Class customer service experience is encouraged rather than impeded.

For example, if I were the operations manager at this café, the priorities I would have Smart Tasked would have been safety, then the customer's comfort and service, and then other support tasks such as cleaning. I would have engrained this order of priorities into every employee's thought process. This way, the barista in question would have naturally realized that cleaning fingerprints and dusting the bottom shelf of the display case was not a safety hazard, so providing the customer with World-Class customer service should have superseded the task.

Fresh Entrée:
From Doughnuts to Smart Tasking Dollars

Far too often, the list of required tasks for Frontline Employees increases—without an evaluation of possible negative affects this could have on their ability to deliver a World-Class customer service experience. Though these tasks all seem important and vital to the success of the operation, when there are too many of them or some are obscure, they can end up hurting the customer service experience. This happens when the number of tasks overwhelms the employee and the employee simply does not have the time, space, or flexibility to prioritize without disrespecting the customer and diminishing the service level.

Smart Tasking is the answer to balancing important tasks and providing a positive customer experience because it ensures that the delivery of World-Class customer service remains the number one priority, except if a safety hazard exists. Then the priority becomes taking care of the safety hazard, immediately followed by a return to delivering the experience and then on to completing the supporting task(s). Remember, if the operation is not kept safe for the employees and the customers, then it becomes impossible to deliver a World-Class customer experience.

All tasks and processes, in the end, are done for the customer, the lady or gentleman who gives you his or her cash in exchange for a product or service. If the task or process isn't good enough for the customer, why bother?

Smart Tasking enables an operation to:
- Provide a World-Class customer service experience.

- Remove unnecessary work and complexity from the operation.

- Make day-to-day life easier, more exciting, and meaningful for Frontline Employees.

- Establish and ensure that the right balance (including timing) exists between delivering a World-Class customer service experience and completing the supporting task(s).

- Provide a structured and prescribed process for getting task(s) completed while allowing flexibility in their completion.

- Increase sales and productivity, which leads to a healthier bottom line.

Managers should review tasks periodically to ensure that they are appropriate and add value to the customer experience.

Let me tell you about my good friends at what was once Wall Street's darling doughnut company. It was America's sweetheart doughnut chain, and I was one of their biggest fans. The joint was touted as the best doughnut business around. Their trademark and secret weapon, the "hot light" in the window, beckoned doughnut lovers far and wide to admire their deep-fried lovelies just as they emerged from 475 degree trans-fatty cooking oil. People (myself included, I must admit) adored these fresh doughnuts.

The company rode a wave of popularity for years and years. In fact, when a new store would open, lines for doughnuts would be blocks long. And then someone popped its bubble. That someone was named Atkins.

The millennium brought in a new dieting mentality and the arrival of the trendy Atkins diet. This diet, which soon became a fad, eschews carbs in any form, including, to sugar-lovers' chagrin, doughnuts. The doughnut company's world would never be the same: the Atkins diet was their worst nightmare. People were now encouraged to forfeit carbs (e.g., doughnuts) in favor of limitless amounts of protein (e.g., bacon). Go figure.

Millions dropped twenty, thirty, fifty, sixty pounds, their fingers dripping with bacon grease instead of doughnut grease. (Although it's likely around the same number gained the weight right back after realizing this frightfully unbalanced diet became hard to sustain over a long period of time.) As time progressed, the company's stock plummeted and it reached the brink of bankruptcy. The CEO actually came out and acknowledged that the Atkins Diet was the cause of his company's downward spiral.

Not one to jump on a dieting bandwagon, I continued to eat doughnuts. One day I approached the doughnut store counter—and this was at the height of the Atkins Diet revolution—and the cashier gave me the upselling spiel she had been taught to recite. I ordered six doughnuts, and she said to me, "You know, you can get a dozen for two dollars more."

I was thinking, *Now, if people are purchasing less and less of your product because they want to consume fewer carbs, why would you continue to upsell more carbs once you get them through the door?* What I would have done if I were the CEO of this doughnut company would be to revise the cashier's task and have her focus on upselling other items sold at the store. For example, "Would you like to add a cup of our delicious coffee for 50 cents extra?" or "Would you like a carton of milk to wash those down?" Smart Tasking is about adjusting to a changing environment.

In order for Smart Tasking to be successful, everyone in the organization must understand why a new policy is important to the success of the operation and when it should be implemented.

Not too long ago, I was asked to visit a large convenience store chain based in the southern part of the US and witness them overhauling the way they do retailing. I'll call the store "Tweetie's 24/7." Tweetie's leadership team was busy reestablishing tasks and instruction templates for every facet of the business. They trained employees on the new duties and presented a checklist of items that needed to be checked off as they completed each task. Sounds nice enough, right?

Well, Tweetie's also instilled within each employee nothing less than the fear of God. Regional managers threatened local managers and employees with their jobs if they didn't comply with the rules and complete all tasks to perfection. I'll never forget my first visit to one of the Tweetie's 24/7 franchises. I was observing a Frontline Employee as she counted a box of individually wrapped candy. The box held one hundred pieces of candy, each with a retail value of 25 cents. The employee dumped out all the contents of the box of candy onto the counter to start her count.

When I asked her what she was doing, she said this was one of the items she had to count every day, check off her list, and see if any of the candies were stolen. As she performed her counting task she was also expected to wait on customers, so you can imagine that this simple count took an exaggerated amount of time to complete.

She said to me with a sneer on her face, "I don't know why I have to count these every day. The count rarely changes because so few people like this flavor and they hardly ever sell."

Some employees decided to go along with the new "improvements," others elected to leave. C-level execs told regional managers and regional managers told local managers that once training was over, the business would undergo an inspection/white glove process. This was enough to make the face of every person employed at Tweetie's turn white as a glove with fear. Employees were also told that if their location failed the evaluation, the store would be in trouble. Deep trouble.

Employees were afraid of losing their jobs. They worked day and night to make sure each was checking off tasks, one by one. When the inspection/white glove process was completed, workers told me it felt like a ton of bricks had been lifted off their shoulders.

I revisited a few Tweetie's 24/7 locations after the inspection/white glove process had been completed and the storm water had been allowed to settle. I was not surprised to find that each store had reverted back to its original state before the revamping. No unnecessary tasks, no checklists. I spoke with several of the operating managers and the feedback I received from each echoed the same theme: "I don't know why we had to do all those new things. I don't see where it helps the business or the customer."

Somewhere along the line, someone forgot to include the reasons, rationale, and customer impact that all these painstaking tasks and processes were supposed to have on the business. When employees understand the reason and rationale they are more likely to embrace and own these tasks and processes, which leads to greater execution. How were these protocols going to ensure a better shopping experience for the customer? If you can't answer that yourself as a decision-maker, how is a Frontline Employee supposed to? Maybe that's your red light that they don't benefit anyone at all.

It's only when people understand the reasoning behind a new strategy—and believe that it can make a difference—that they will embrace and sustain the processes. Fear Tasking is not Smart Tasking. Fear only delivers short-term results, nothing more.

If you're ever tempted to motivate your Frontline Employees through fear, think about this first:

**Human beings naturally flee from fear;
never do they embrace it.**

I have provided a few negative examples of where Smart Tasking was sorely needed but not implemented. Being an essentially positive person, I'd like to leave you with an example of an organization that implemented Smart Tasking with dramatically successful results.

Marvelous Meals, Inc. operated most of the food service stores at the Atlanta, Georgia airport. I was assigned to the Atlanta business unit to improve airport operations, and after two weeks of observation I noticed that although businesses officially closed at 11:00 PM, operations really began shutting down around 9:00 PM, at least from a customer perspective, as the level of service was near rock bottom and the product selection was scaled back, even though the hours of operation stated the closing time as 11:00 PM. In reality, the message being communicated was, "Yes, our doors are open until 11:00 PM, but the great customer service ends at 9:00 PM."

Once the clock struck 9:00 PM, everyone shifted their focus from serving customers to getting their areas cleaned and prepped for the close of business. I discovered that Frontline Employees couldn't stay past 11:00 PM because they weren't allowed any overtime. When passengers from the nightly 9:45 PM flight in from Dallas, always a packed flight, came through the airport, they could never buy anything. Employees were too busy following the 11:00 PM mandate to offer any assistance.

After a month, I could clearly see from the transaction logs and sales data that revenues were substantially lower between 9:00 and 11:00 PM than at other hours. During that two-hour period, dollar amounts were 60 to 70 percent below normal two-hour time periods.

Frontline Employees knew they had certain tasks they had to complete before 11:00 PM, but nobody had ever put on paper the most effective and efficient way to perform the task, or the recommended time in which the task should be completed, realizing that some flexibility needed to exist when the recommended time might impede the customer experience. For example, if a delayed flight caused a non-customer peak time to become a customer peak time, this might slightly alter the recommended time for the completion of the task.

To the employees, it made sense to rush through all these tasks during the last two hours of the shift. I told them not to do everything in two hours. There were several small, pre-9:00 PM lulls, and we started spreading close-down processes throughout these lull periods without sacrificing the customer experience.

Within thirty days, the Operations Manager said, "What's going on here? Is something wrong? We never do that dollar range between 9:00 and 11:00 PM." I explained that Frontline Employees didn't previously have proper processes in place and hadn't understood the effect this was having on customers. The Operations Manager responded with some flak, as he had been there twelve years. He felt the need to be the originator of any successful new ideas.

The Operations Manager finally said it wasn't right for me to institute changes without first getting his approval, but he allowed them to stay in place. Frontline Employees liked the changes because they resulted in less stress. More importantly, they no longer saw customers as a distraction. The airport shops simply needed to balance providing customer service with completing other necessary tasks.

Before you launch your own Smart Tasking initiative, take note of these suggested steps:

1. Understand the operation and what it takes to deliver operational soundness.

2. Identify the right tasks from the beginning and then involve Frontline Employees in the process.

3. Prescribe appropriate times for tasks to be completed, keeping in mind that the more customer-intrusive tasks should be completed during off-peak time.

4. Do not sacrifice safety in the process of prioritizing tasks; the operation must be kept safe.

5. Support each task with a simple, thorough, and easy-to-execute set of instructions.

6. Dry-run the tasks and evaluate whether the completion of these tasks impedes the customer experience.

7. Don't be afraid to make adjustments.

8. Review tasks periodically to see if they are still appropriate according to a changing environment (e.g. seasonal changes, holidays, peak season).

9. Provide training that includes reasons and rationales for tasks, such as the importance of not allowing tasks to impede the customer experience and the smartest way to complete tasks.

As a side note, after our initial success at Smart Tasking at the airport, the addition of two new pieces of in-store equipment required us to make changes to accommodate the new equipment without disrupting the timing of employee tasks versus customer flow. The situation wound up being a win/win as the sales for those two hours held up, even when we extracted out the additional time needed to maintain the new equipment.

Another great benefit was touted by other airport employees who could now benefit from the entire customer service offering, as many of them ended their shift from other operations in the airport at 10:00 PM. They came off shift desperate for good food, refreshing beverages, and some great service.

"Companies simply must solve the service puzzle—they have no choice not to," reports business consulting firm Accenture in *The Customer Service Challenge: Creating the "Perfect" Customer Call*. "If they don't, their disenchanted, frustrated customers will become even easier prey for competitors. The service bar is being raised across all industries, causing customers to hold any product or service provider to the same high standards as service leaders."

Remember, delivering a poor customer experience to the customer is like putting him in your car and driving him to the front door of your competitor... who, by the way, is waiting with open arms.

Temperature Check

Take a second to reflect on these questions:

1. Who developed the Frontline Employees' current tasks/ processes?

2. When was the last time these tasks/processes were reviewed?

3. What do the Frontline employees think about the tasks/ processes?

4. Have you ever talked to customers about the experience they receive?

5. Do the current tasks/processes impede or enable the delivery of a world-class customer experience?

6. Do you ever gather feedback on the processes/tasks that are in place?

6.5. Do you think Smart Tasking is important? If so, what next step will you take to make a fresh change?

These questions are a bit more open-ended than the Temperature Check questions at the end of the last chapter, but as a general guideline, the answers to 4, 6, and 6.5 should all be "yes." You should know who developed your Frontline Employees' current tasks and processes. Tasks and processes should have been reviewed recently and viewed positively by the employees carrying them out, and the delivery of World-Class customer service should be enabled.

You should be regularly taking customer feedback.

If all of these answers closely match your answers, then congratulations, you have prepared a well-done Smart Tasking operation that is ready to serve! If not, it's probably time to add a little seasoning and put it back in the oven for a while.

What's your Temperature? Smart Tasking

Temperature	Correct Response Rate	Explanation
Rare	0 correct Temperature Check responses	Where did these frontline tasks come from? Who knows, but they must be there for a reason, or maybe not!
Medium Rare	1-2 correct Temperature Check responses	There is some rhyme and reason to how frontline tasks are developed and assigned, but they are probably not often updated or reviewed, to the aggravation of employees and customers.
Medium	3-4 correct Temperature Check responses	Frontline tasks are periodically reviewed and updated by top executives, stakeholders, and other decision-makers, but you're missing out on crucial frontline feedback.
Medium Well	5-6 correct Temperature Check responses	Frontline tasks are documented, reviewed, and updated, taking the current needs of employees and customers into account. But there may still be some "legacy" tasks impeding delivery of World-Class customer experience, or reviews may not be frequent or thorough enough.
Well Done	**6.5 correct Temperature Check responses**	No frontline task is assigned or performed unless it passes a rigorous documentation and review process that includes substantial feedback from employees and customers. Reviews are frequent and thorough, with quick, decisive action.

*Keep checking the temperature to make sure you get to Well Done and stay there

Actually, you have kept your customers waiting for Fresh Customer Service long enough; put it in the microwave so that your Frontline Employees are equipped and empowered to deliver a World-Class customer experience now.

Fresh Technologies:
Shelf Tracking

Think back to the beleaguered Tweetie's 24/7 employee who dutifully counted individually wrapped candies that were rarely purchased to make sure none were stolen. By using automated shelf-tracking systems, retailers can easily maintain a constant count of goods that are on the shelves, in the back room, and in the warehouse.

Armed with a wirelessly-enabled personal digital assistant (PDA), an employee can scan product barcodes to quickly count inventory levels of a specific product. This data can then instantly be transmitted throughout the retail enterprise and even to outside partners, such as shippers or suppliers. In addition, retailers can use this data to easily track items that are sitting on the shelves for long periods of time, or maybe disappearing without explanation!

 **News Fresh**

In September of 2006, after suffering huge setbacks from failed batteries to lagging sales, Dell CEO Kevin Rollins unveiled a new strategy called Dell 2.0, which featured a heavier emphasis on customer service and long-term relationships, and less reliance on Dell's traditional aggressive pricing as a way of winning market share. An article in E-*Commerce Times* paraphrased Rollins: "…Dell would look for ways to grow the firm's services business, launching a customer service push known as DellConnect meant to enable the company to meet a customer's needs more quickly." Rollins also expressed Dell's revised commitment to invest $150 million to upgrade the customer service experience, which has been Dell's bête-noire and source of intense criticism in the last few years. I commend Dell for realizing the root of their problem: a corroded customer service experience in need of a fresh overhaul.

 **Fresh Bit**

To get a free and helpful tool to help you develop balanced processes and tasks for your team, visit **www.themichaeld-brown.com**. While you're there, drop me a line on my blog or send me an email on any experiences that you might have had where the employee was more focused on another duty/ task as opposed to taking care of you.

Take Out

1. Smart Tasking efforts need to be balanced between performing important tasks and serving the needs of the customer. Keeping a clean store is important, but not to the point it should cause unbearably long lines at the checkout counter. Safety of customers and Frontline Employees always needs to be the first priority, but after that is taken care of, priorities need to be set in a manner that is respectful of the customer's limited time and busy schedule. Remember that all tasks and processes, in the end, are done for the customer, who keeps you in business. The tasks/processes need to aid, not impede, the delivery of a World-Class customer service experience.

2. Human beings naturally flee from fear; never do they embrace it. Fear Tasking is not Smart Tasking. Fear only delivers short-term results, nothing more. When implementing Smart Tasking at your organization, carefully review the tasks Frontline Employees carry out and perform an honest assessment of what motivates them to complete these tasks: Is it a sense of involvement and empowerment in the workplace, or is it simple fear of punishment and/or termination of employment if tasks are not carried out?

3. Make sure the "fun factor" is not overlooked when developing frontline tasks. Obviously Frontline Employees cannot expect to have fun all day, but properly executed Smart Tasking can make day-to-day life easier and more exciting and meaningful (i.e., fun) for them. Performing periodic assessments to ensure the balance of frontline tasks ensures they are appropriate and add value to the customer experience, which makes things more "fun" for customers and employees alike!

Fresh Step ③
Make-It-Right Power

Fresh Appetizer: No Love for the Customer
at Loveseats, Inc. and the Gold Standard

"It's not me. It's corporate." The night I heard this pathetic, all-too common excuse for a poor customer experience will be etched into my memory of customer service nightmares forever.

It was a Friday evening in early June. The Southern California air was light with a warm breeze. I was happily on my way to the grocery store to pick up a loaf of fresh gourmet bread to accompany dinner when I stumbled upon a sign in front of the local branch of a huge national furniture retailer which I'll call "Loveseats, Inc." The sign in the window read, "20 percent off any single item."

After having paid $3.67 a gallon to fill up my car earlier that day, I was in the mood for a discount on anything I could get—even though I didn't need any new furniture. In other words, I was an impulse shopper on a whim who hadn't done any serious planning or research beforehand. I was the ideal customer.

For some time, however, I had been toying with the idea of buying a new bed for my guest bedroom. Though I was sentimental about the old one—it was my first bed after college and a reminder of how far I had come (after all, in those days my diet consisted of the signature college meal of Ramen Noodle, now I could actually afford gourmet bread)— it was in miserable shape. My college bed was leaning at an unsightly angle, which said very little of my capabilities in hospitality. What would visiting college buddies think when they saw that familiar bed? That I'm cheap? Clueless?

And so the little devil on my shoulder convinced me how great a stylish new bed would look in the guest room. I picked up my bread from Traders Joe's (who, by they way, treated me like a gourmet customer and provided a great shopping experience from the front door to the bread aisle and on to the checkout stand) and then stopped by Loveseats on my way home to investigate the sale sign that I had seen earlier in the evening.

When I walked into this behemoth of a furniture store I felt like I had entered the Minotaur's Furniture Labyrinth—beds, dressers, desks, and chairs stretched as far as the eye could see down long, limitless aisles. The sheer size and unending options intimidated me and I was immediately lost, confused, and without a clue as to where the ideal bed for the guest room would be.

I wandered around for quite some time and bumped into a few inconspicuous lampshades, all the while noticing that the eight salespeople huddled around the desk watching TV and folding paper airplanes weren't going to interrupt their festivities on my behalf. And mind you, a bad day shopping in a furniture store for me is forty-six seconds versus forty-five. The staff just glanced at me with looks on their faces as if to say, "Oh my goodness, a customer," but none bothered to assist me.

After ten minutes of this hopeless wandering, a salesperson with a nametag reading "Sharon" finally approached and offered help. I told Sharon I was looking for a dark-colored bed similar to one that I had seen at a friend's house. The impatient look on Sharon's face simply stated, *Come on, guy, give me a little more information. I've never been to your friend's house and don't know what kind of bed he has.*

She walked me around the store and showed me my options. Evidently, the one I liked didn't come in the color that

I wanted. My second choice was too big for the guest room. We wandered around a bit more and finally found one that I kind of fancied, but it was (of course) more expensive than all the others, costing more than I wanted to pay.

Sharon said to me, "You know we have a 20 percent off sale. So you'll get 20 percent off this bed."

"OK, that's good," I said with a victorious smile.

"Do you have a Loveseats, Inc. card?" Sharon asked me.

"I haven't used my Loveseats, Inc. card in several years," I replied. "The account is probably closed."

"Well," said Sharon, "if you don't use your Loveseats, Inc. card, we will give you another 10 percent off."

In amazement and confusion, I asked, "Why would you give me a discount for not using your store card?"

"You see, the card is really through a credit card company, and they charge us a large percentage to process it," Sharon said. "So normally we don't even ask the customers if they want to use their Loveseats, Inc. card, and therefore we don't push it either."

I'm standing there thinking to myself, *Why even have a store card if you don't want your customers to use it? And do I really need to know all of this information?*

So we picked out a bed, Sharon did some math in her head, and told me the price. Wow, was I getting a good deal—20 percent off and 10 percent for promising not to use my Love-seats, Inc. card ... I was sold! She brought the price sign over to the computer and started to type in my information.

Even though I was getting a good deal, I still wasn't jazzed about the style of the bed. So I said to Sharon, "Let me check the store next door before I make my decision." She agreed. I didn't find what I was looking for at the other store, so I returned a few minutes later to complete the transaction.

"Do you really think this is a good deal?" I asked her.

"Yes, Mr. Brown," she said. "It's rare to get 20 percent off, and plus, you're getting another 10 percent off."

She continued to enter the item into the computer. The original delivery date was no longer available because in the midst of my hesitation someone else had taken that delivery spot.

So I agreed to receive the bed a week later than originally expected. Sharon continued to key in my information. Click, click, click, *beeeeeeep.* Sharon entered the bed into the computer, but the computer responded with the most unwelcoming, prolonged "beep." After a few minutes Sharon said, "Oh, I am going to have to get my manager. The computer is only giving you the discount off one piece of the bed."

Sharon went to talk to the manager. About five minutes later she returned and said, "Mr. Brown, I'm sorry. My manager just informed me that the 20 percent is only for the highest priced item."

Confused, I replied, "What are you talking about? I'm only buying one bed."

"I know what you mean," she said. "The computer breaks down the bed into many parts."

"You must be kidding me," I said, my jaw hanging wide open. "The sign states only one price for the completed bed."

"I'm sorry," she said. "I didn't know."

I asked her for the hard copy of the advertisement that stated 20 percent off any single item. Another salesperson came up while we were talking.

"Yeah, I know what you mean," said the salesman, whose nametag read "Jason." "It seems like a bed is a bed and is one single item, but they break the bed down and only give the discount on one piece." Jason advised me to talk to the manager.

As I was waiting for the manager, several salespeople who were standing around nearby flying paper airplanes did nothing to help the situation, except maybe provide a great distraction. (*Obviously*, I thought to myself, *this place is over-staffed, and a World-Class customer service experience is the last thing on their minds. Although these salespeople could probably provide a World-Class experience in flying paper airplanes.*) I finally was escorted to speak with the manager, who sat behind a large mahogany desk in a corner office.

"How can I help you?" the manager, named Linda, asked.

"I've been in here for forty-five minutes and was sold on a purchase that I was told would come with a 20 percent discount, plus another 10 percent discount for not using my store credit card," I said.

"I'm sorry, there is nothing I can do," Linda said, with an urgent sense of faux empathy. "The computer is locked down. We can't change anything. This sale has been going on for two weeks. Customers have been getting confused with the 20 percent off, and some stores are overriding the computer and giving them the discount. Many stores got in trouble and corporate cracked down on them, and this store was one of them. So that's why no one will give you the discount—they are afraid of losing their jobs."

"I understand what you're saying," I replied, "but nowhere on the price sign did I see the bed broken into five pieces with individual price points. I saw one price, and the salesperson sold me the bed as one item—which I believe to be correct—with the stated discount."

And here she spoke those five words, nice enough on their own yet pure evil when combined:
"It's not me. It's corporate."

"Let me get this straight," I said. "There's nothing you can do?"

"No, there is nothing I can do," Linda said.

I thanked Linda for her time, thanked Sharon, and walked out as fast as I could before one of the paper airplanes hit me in the face.

What's wrong with this story? Did I hear you say "everything"? Well, I agree. Allow me to elaborate. Linda the manager said the sale had been going on for two weeks and customers were confused. She even stated many salespeople were overriding the computer and giving the discount against company policy.

When corporate realized this was happening, and that there was indeed a problem, why didn't they provide a solution that would empower the Frontline Employee to make the customer happy—as opposed to just locking down the computer?

Why didn't anyone tell Sharon how the 20 percent discount worked? After all, she was not a new employee, she stated that she had been at that location for three years, so she should have been familiar with how the computer broke the bed down into multiple pieces and explained it to me before we started the transaction.

Shouldn't there have been a review of the promotion after it was executed in the field by the Frontline Employees? Someone should have listened to the Frontline Employees about the confusion and made it right. And if this couldn't have happened, the Frontline Employees should have been given Make-It-Right Power themselves, so that in these kinds of circumstances, they could override the computer or be provided with an alternative method to make up for this misleading advertisement. In this way, you can guarantee that the customer is satisfied and leaves with a reason to sing your praises and be a walking billboard for your company…and that the employee doesn't feel helpless and backed into an uncomfortable corner.

The best solution in this situation would be to have a "sales execution review meeting" on the first day the sale started. This meeting would serve as a mechanism to fully explain the sale, potential problems that might be encountered, and any possible solutions that the Frontline Employee should implement if problems did arise.

On that warm evening at Loveseats, Inc., neither the employee nor the manager was empowered. They let me walk out with my dollars in my pocket. Now I understand why there weren't many customers in the store and why I saw no sales transactions taking place.

When all was said and done I went home, turned on my computer, and quickly pulled up the Loveseats, Inc. website. Looking at it, one would think that the aforementioned scene was impossible. Their homepage is painted with the testimonials of loyal and satisfied customers. Loveseats, Inc. also invites you to apply for their store credit card. And yes, Loveseats, Inc. invites you to print off a coupon for 20 percent off any single item.

I've included the actual marketing content of their website, which is as follows:
It's all about finding what's right for you.
What fits your lifestyle?
What feels right for you?
Whether you're shopping for a sofa or a job,

at the new Loveseats, Inc. you can feel the love.
Feel the commitment to satisfying customers.
Feel the pride in our company and coworkers.
Feel the love for the furniture we sell.

On the web, in our stores and offices at Loveseats, Inc. you...
FEEL THE LOVE
20% OFF any regular price single item

Needless to say, I did not feel the love that day at Loveseats, Inc.

Make-It-Right Power puts the ability to deliver a World-Class customer service experience in the hands of the people who are best able to deliver it: The employees who interact with the customers, be it in person, on the phone, online chat/Instant Messaging, email, or snail mail. It's about empowering and positioning employees to be able to instantly solve customer problems and view them as opportunities to Make-It-Right now for the customer.

Why is Make-It-Right Power important?

Nine times out of ten, a customer problem starts with a simple issue that can be solved in a matter of minutes. For instance, at Loveseats, Inc., the manager should have been able to override the computer and give me the promised one-item discount. But most policies and procedures, much like this one, have conditioned employees to go into "protect the company's assets mode" as soon as the customer begins to state his or her problem.

We have either knowingly or unknowingly put our employees in defensive mode when a customer states a problem and the employee has not been given basic power to Make-It-Right. This defensive mode only serves to exacerbate the problem, which could have been just an average, simple problem, into a gigantic problem of mammoth proportions that could be the defining factor of whether the customer will be one for life or one who never returns again and tells everyone he knows of the horrible experience he had.

Customers want to know that employees will genuinely hear them out and empathize with them—but mostly, and above all, they want to see an instant solution to their problem. Make-It-Right Power delivers both the responsibility and the prescribed authority to the employees to transform a customer's bad experience into a positive one, or in the best case scenario, one that can proactively hedge off the situation as a result of prescribed Make-It-Right Power before it can fester into a bad experience.

One of my most admired hotel chains is the Ritz-Carlton Hotel Company. Their focus on employees and customers is the epitome of world-class. The Ritz-Carlton has a set of Gold Standards. It is these standards that constitute the core and foundation of the Ritz-Carlton.

According to the Ritz-Carlton, "The Gold Standards encompass the values and philosophy by which we operate." Part of these Gold Standards is a concept they call "Service Values." Service Values is a list of twelve employee commitments that start with "I."

One of the twelve is "I own and immediately resolve guest problems." If you walk up to a Ritz Carlton employee, he will have a little card in one of his pockets that reminds him of the Gold Standards. Employees are given an up-to-a-certain-dollar amount of hotel funds that they can commit to delivering instant resolutions to guests' problems. Regardless of what industry you are in, you too can empower your Frontline Employees (remember frontline includes anyone who interacts with customers in person, on the phone, or via online chat/IM, email, or snail mail) with the knowledge and tools to own and immediately solve customer problems.

Fresh Entrée:
Buon Appetito Café's Frontline Heroes

I worked for a growing deli chain I will call Buon Appetito Café that decided to alter their menu offering in a particular market and include more premium sandwiches. Now let me remind you that the customers in this market were happy with a sandwich that consisted of meat, bread, cheese, mayonnaise, mustard, and no more than a half-serving of vegetables (perhaps a small lettuce leaf and a tomato slice). Nevertheless, someone made the decision to offer fewer traditional sandwiches and more gourmet sandwiches.

For example, one gourmet sandwich included focaccia bread, arugula, pesto, red onions, lettuce, tomato, roasted peppers, feta cheese, and cucumbers. I am still trying to figure out how someone thought this would satisfy customers who barely wanted lettuce and tomato on their sandwiches.

The Frontline Employees were told to talk up the new gourmet sandwiches and get customers to purchase them. You can only imagine the complaints that the Frontline Employees received from the customers, who overnight saw the disappearance of their "simple" sandwiches and the appearance of gourmet sandwiches that had names and ingredients that were foreign to them.

People had different perceptions of what the sandwiches would taste like. The names and ingredients didn't meet the expectations of their taste buds. After all, I don't think they had ever eaten many of these ingredients before.

When the Frontline Employees received the complaints, they felt a bit helpless and figured the easiest solution would be to issue a full refund and hope that would fulfill their requirement to make the customer happy. In order to issue a full refund, they would have to call the manager over to issue the refund. In many cases, after receiving a refund, the customer was still going on about their disappointment in the new sandwich. In many cases the customers just needed to vent, needed validation of their disappointment, and wanted to be heard.

I saw several problems here: The employees needed another method for making the customer happy besides just issuing a refund, the customer still wasn't totally happy with a refund, the customer experience for both the complaining customer and the customer waiting to be served was diminished, the productivity of the Frontline Employees and the managers was diminished because an employee had to stop serving other customers to summon a manager and the manager was making a number of trips during the day to approve refunds, and the business was not offering samplings of the products so that customers could try the new sandwiches before they purchased them. My task was to solve these identified problems.

One of my first recommendations was to assign levels of authority. I recommended that senior Frontline Employees receive six "customer satisfaction dollars," and that non-senior Frontline Employees receive five "customer satisfaction dollars." If they could resolve a problem for under six dollars or five dollars (this would take care of the average customer's purchase), as the case may have been, they were given the power to make it happen. The customer would sign off on a slip, minimizing the time a manager was disrupted. This kept customers, who still had their complaints validated and addressed, happy, and it kept operations moving.

The initial corporate response to the customer satisfaction dollar idea was, "The employees will abuse it; we shouldn't give them that much power." But documentation (employees had to turn in the receipt and a signed customer slip) kept employee abuse to a minimum, and customers were sufficiently wowed by the service they were getting to not try to take advantage of the program.

The first phrase out of an employee's mouth was, "What can I do to make you happy," and some customers said, "I just want a refund." Now, the problem with just supplying a refund was that the customer might still be frustrated and not return to the store. However, the employees also had the power to offer a one-dollar coupon that a customer could use on their next visit, and this "cherry on top" really impressed the guest.

Some customers said, "Oh, I just wanted to let you know what I thought." In many of these cases, the employee would offer the one-dollar coupon and ask them to please give Buon Appetito Café another opportunity to make a sandwich that they would like. Frontline Employees were given the power to "make it right," and the customer satisfaction index increased. And now that Frontline Employees, who were previously powerless when a manager was busy or out, could help a customer who simply wanted to vent or have a minor problem resolved, the bottom line improved.

We're not trying to do the impossible with the customer; we're just allowing them to have as many problems as possible resolved with a minimum of pain and aggravation on both the customer and employee sides of the equation.

The following are steps to giving Frontline Employees Make-It-Right Power:

1. Spend some time (throughout the entire business day) with the Frontline Employees to understand how they currently solve customers' problems.

2. Find out from the employees what would make it easier for them to solve these problems.

3. Record this gathered knowledge into a "best practice document."

4. Establish Make-it-Right authority for every employee in the organization.

5. Define a policy and procedure around how to administer Make-It-Right Power. Keep it simple and fun!

6. Provide the necessary training.

It's important to establish levels of authority with every employee so that they know what they are authorized to do when certain problems arise with customers. For example, if you're a Frontline Employee, you may be empowered to solve a customer's problem up to a prescribed dollar amount, with an in-store incentive, or a gift card, or whatever other mechanism may be in place.

As an organizational leader, you need to be clear if this empowerment is the same for all levels of the organization, or if it differs based on the position of the employee. It is not uncommon for a General Manager to be empowered to a greater degree than a Frontline Employee.

A clear set of guidelines needs to accompany Make-It-Right Power. These instructions would include how the employees will administer the solutions to the customer's problems, what documentation should be completed, and a check-and-balance system for the manager. It does not behoove us to come up with a robust empowerment tool without providing clear training to the employees who will need to administer it. Therefore, simple training should be administered that will discuss the rationale behind Make-It-Right Power, including its administration and its checks and balances.

Temperature Check

This chapter's temperature check is a little different than the ones in preceding chapters. Now that we've thoroughly examined Make-It-Right Power and how its presence or absence impacts customer service, review your own organization's customer service experience to see if Make-It-Right Power is present or absent.

Make a list of commonly encountered customer service problems at your organization in the first column in the chart below. Then discuss what your company's policy is, if any, for responding to these problems in the middle column. Then write down any suggested improvements you have for solving these problems in order to provide a World-Class customer service experience in the last column.

Current Problems	Prescribed Solutions	Suggested Improvements
Example: The flight that John was on from Chicago to Phoenix was late taking off because of fueling issues. John arrived in Phoenix too late for his connecting flight and would have to take a flight that was scheduled two hours later, at midnight. John has been traveling all day and is visibly exhausted. John also wants some compensation for this screw-up.	**Example**: Book John on the midnight flight, and offer him the 800 customer resolution center phone number that he can call tomorrow.	**Example**: Provide John with a $10 voucher that he can use to purchase a drink and a snack at the airport. Issue John a $100 travel voucher that he can use to book a future flight.

Take one or more of the preceding suggested improvements that you have just written and turn it into a policy or procedure that will lead to the empowerment of the Frontline Employee and will equip him with the power to Make-It-Right Now. This document should spell out what's appropriate for employees at various levels in the organization.

You should also provide an idea of what training is needed and how it would be delivered to the Frontline Employees. Once all columns in this chart are completely filled with ideas that everyone in the organization can agree upon and that have been proven to work with your customers, you will have yourself a well-done helping of Make-It-Right Power!

 **Fresh Technologies**

An increasing number of organizations are taking advantage of software systems that automate human resources (HR) processes. Employees are given personalized, Web-based access to information such as benefits and pay, scheduling of hours and time off, internal promotions or transfer opportunities, and training documents.

A "Make-It-Right" document can be made instantly available via the Internet to all employees across the organization. Frontline employees can be provided with inexpensive "dumb" PC terminals in the break room so they can have access to this important document when they need it most: during the workday. By allowing employees to email suggestions for improvements or additions, you can create a "living" Make-It-Right document that keeps pace with the development of new and unforeseen customer problems!

 **News Fresh**

A study performed by Bain & Co. found that executives and customers have drastically different opinions of customer service. The study cites that 80 percent of executives feel they are doing an outstanding job of serving customers, while a paltry 8 percent of customers agree. According to Bain, every four years the average company can lose up to half its customers. Aggressive pricing (on hotel phone bills, credit card fees, and rental-car gas charges, to name a few examples) has increased.

In *Fortune Magazine*, Bain's Fred Reichheld said such aggressive pricing has increased as the profit pressure on companies has intensified; yet, he says abusing customers this way only "destroys the future of a business." He believes that this unrelenting behavior, "and not scandals like Enron and Tyco," is why fewer than half of all Americans could say anything nice about large companies.

So what's the bottom line? In my own opinion, leaders and decision-makers in these organizations have failed to keep their eyes on the prize: the customer. And the only way to do this is by serving Fresh Customer Service through empowered Frontline Employees who have the authority and know-how to resolve customer problems on the spot.

 **Take Out**

1. Since Frontline Employees typically encounter and discover customer problems, they should be equipped and enabled with the Make-It-Right Power necessary to resolve them. This makes the frontline experience run more smoothly and efficiently for both customers and Frontline Employees. Involve Frontline Employees from the beginning of your efforts to develop Make-It-Right Power. What problems do they see, what solutions do they think will work?

2. Establish a robust, formalized Make-It-Right Power training program. Don't be so rigorous or formal that the experience becomes a chore for the Frontline Employees or that you lose the ability to adapt training to changing needs of employees and customers. Involve employees in designing the training program and take their feedback. However, don't get so loose with training that Make-It-Right Power becomes part of your organization's "unwritten rules" or something new employees are expected to pick up by osmosis.

3. Put firm, well-documented policies and procedures in place so that Frontline Employees don't go awry in their efforts to resolve customer problems with Make-It-Right Power. For example, Buon Appetito Café limited how

many customer satisfaction dollars Frontline Employees could distribute based on their level of authority, and also required sufficient documentation any time customer satisfaction dollars were distributed.

Fresh Step ❹
The What-If Arsenal

Fresh Appetizer: Living After Midnight,
            Gas Pains, Cash & Carry

Several years ago, I was working on a project that had me flying twice a week between my home in Southern California
and the job site in Northern California. In order to keep my
mind off of the grueling travel, to say nothing of maintaining my sanity, I'd make small talk with airline employees.

Etched in my mind is one conversation that I had with Jake,
a Frontline Employee who worked at the counter of a large
airline at Oakland International Airport. Jake asked me
what I did for a living, and I told him I help organizations
and individuals create World-Class customer service experi-

ences. He looked puzzled, so I simply said, "I teach people how to make customers happy."

"Well, you can't make all customers happy," Jake said. He looked at me with an expression that said, *What do you have to say to that?*

"What do you mean you can't make all customers happy?" I countered.

"Let me tell you about a customer I had to deal with last night," said Jake. "A few weeks ago, the customer purchased a ticket to fly on Thursday at 12 a.m.—midnight. He showed up at 11:00 p.m. on Thursday thinking he was going to board a flight in an hour. I had to explain to him that he was supposed to be here the night before (Wednesday) to catch his midnight flight—since the coming midnight that night was actually the beginning of the day on Friday. The customer got angry with me and failed to understand why he couldn't take the next flight. I told him that the flight that was about to leave in one hour, at midnight, is really the midnight Friday flight.

"I continued explaining how it was his own mistake because our reservation desk always makes sure to explain this time scenario," Jake said. "But the customer was furious. Livid. He wanted to know what I could do to fix the situation.

I told him that according to our policy, I would have to charge him a $100 change fee.

"I went on to tell him I would have to check to see if there was availability on tonight's flight and charge him the fare difference for the available class of service—which could be several hundred dollars, since his original ticket was booked 21 days in advance and the ticket he would have to purchase now would be for the same day of travel and therefore more expensive. He became more angry and frustrated, and I simply told him, 'Sir, it's your fault that you didn't read the ticket.'"

Jake looked at me and said, "So what would you tell my company in this case and what would you tell me I should have done differently?"

"First of all, how often does this happen?" I asked.

"It happens all the time," Jake said. "I deal with it almost every night."

That was a blinking red light if I'd ever seen one. I told Jake that in this case I would start by working with the leadership team to understand the root cause of the confusion, especially because numerous customers are showing up for the wrong flights on a regular basis.

Perhaps they could ensure that the reservation agent clearly explains the timing issue to the customer. They could also print in bold, highlighted letters that this is a midnight flight of the day that seems to be one day before you leave, i.e., "Please show up at the airport the day before, on _____ day."

"As far as what you could have done," I told Jake, "I would advise you to start by apologizing to the customer for the confusion and be more empathetic. The customer doesn't need to have salt rubbed into his wound by being reminded of his mistake. I would have also said something like, 'I understand your frustration. Let me see if I can search the computer for the lowest available fare to minimize the cost to you.' At this point, the customer will feel that you care and are at least trying to help him solve the problem while minimizing the financial impact."

I explained to Jake that we must have processes and tools in place to handle scenarios when the customer is upset. I call this a **What-If Arsenal**. A What-If Arsenal should be at an employee's fingertips or stored in his head for instant retrieval when the manager is present and when he's away. Otherwise, you may as well put a sign on the door that reads, "Expect a bad customer experience. The manager is not available, and we don't have the power to make things right."

If Jake had simply reached into his What-If Arsenal (the physical one or the mental one that would have to be lifted from the hard copy and stored in his head) and been more kind to the customer, and done his best to find an economical solution to the conundrum at hand, World-Class customer service would have resulted.

Why is the What-If Arsenal such an important element of a World-Class customer service experience? The What-If Arsenal provides the tools and techniques that help foster a consistently superb business-to-customer interaction. Many customer problems, like the midnight flight confusion at Jake's airline, are repetitive and can be solved with the same solutions that have been used before.

I have two more vignettes that help me explain what happens when the What-If Arsenal is not in place: The first is a classic example about *keeping it fresh* and the second shows how just plain readiness could be the deciding factor between a happy and an infuriated customer.

In July 2005, gas prices reached an all-time high (I know, I know, I'm always griping about gas prices. Doesn't everybody, though?). To my and every Californian's astonishment, prices here for unleaded fuel were tiptoeing over $3.50 a gallon—as opposed to the $1.50 a gallon I was paying while living in Georgia in 1999.

I was traveling through the breathtaking mountains and valleys of California and decided to stop at a gas station (actually, my decision was heavily influenced by my fuel light flashing for the preceding twenty minutes) to begrudgingly fill up my SUV, when I saw an attendant trying to pacify a middle-aged female customer who was upset about the station's gasoline shortage.

For some reason, there was a supply disruption on the West Coast and many stations along this route were out of gas. I started to get a little concerned because I was not going to be able to fill up at this station and get reward points on my credit card. (I think at that time I only needed 100,000 more to qualify for the toaster.)

This employee was fully prepared to deliver a plausible solution to the customer—he was directing everyone off to the nearest competing gas station he thought was not out of fuel. This is exactly the solution the attendant offered the disgruntled customer who was unable to fill up. I heard this lady say that with gas at $3.50 a gallon, she didn't want to drive to another station.

"It's more costly than before to just go to the next gas station," she said, "plus I had planned my route so that I could come here, since this gas station's prices are usually cheaper."

The attendant looked at me and said, "I'm not sure why all the customers are acting this way. Normally, it's not such a problem when we run out of fuel—we just direct them to the nearest station that has fuel."

Sure, customers have usually been okay with a gas shortage. After all, they could just drive to the nearest gas station and buy gas for about the same price from a competitor. Or they could wait an hour until the next delivery truck shows up. However, on this Thursday afternoon, the customers sounded more like rioters. Patience was at a minimum. Gasoline was so expensive that traveling to the nearest competitor would have cost a considerable amount of money and personal time, especially considering the traffic congestions that were present. The attendant's regular solution to please the customer was not good enough. It had become stale.

Now that gas prices are two-and-a-half times 1999's $1.50 per gallon, there needs to be a better, fresher solution to offer the customer—something more than pointing the customer off to the next gas station. Prices are now too high for that to be a valid alternative. But what could the attendant have offered to make the customers more comfortable in this crappy situation?

Let's remember that the root cause of the problem is beyond the operator's hands or the Frontline Employee's hands: There is no way he can predict or alter a supply shortage. But he can come to work equipped and pull from the What-If Arsenal that has been filled by colleagues and managers and stored in his head or in a nearby document for the quick solution retrieval. For a gas station, this What-If Arsenal would factor in an unpredictable gasoline shortage (since it has happened several times before and seems to be a common problem), as well as back-up solutions to make the customer feel better when the unexpected happens.

While I realize that there is little the attendant could have done to make gas appear out of thin air for his customers, he *could* have offered them a cup of coffee or tea, or even a small future discount to brighten their spirits. Because, at a time like this, where emotions are volatile and tempers are slippery, sending customers off to the nearest station is not going to cut it. All it is going to do is make them angrier—and they may be more likely to avoid this gas station in the future.

I remember another time I witnessed a situation when a What-If Arsenal would have prevented a customer service snafu. *Sometimes, you just want your money back*, my friend Tony showed me. I realized this one Sunday afternoon when we were working out at the gym together. Tony was slower than usual and generally unfocused during the workout. I asked him what was wrong and he said his mind was occupied with a run-in that his wife, Lisa, had while returning a set of speakers to a popular electronics store. Lisa didn't like that the speakers lacked a remote control, and she saw a better pair at a competitor.

Lisa was hesitant to take the speakers back because she didn't want to go through the rigmarole of returning them, Tony explained. We continued to work out and about fifteen minutes after he told me this, Tony's mobile phone was buzzing. He stopped working out to answer. It was Lisa. She said when she finally went back to the store, the sales clerk said he couldn't give her a refund for the $178 speakers because he only had $40 in the cash drawer.

Tony started screaming. He really lost it, spewing small saliva droplets of amazement and frustration into the cell phone (I thought, *his poor wife on the other end!*). He insisted on speaking to the sales clerk Lisa was dealing with. Lisa (and I could hear all of this conversation because both of their voices were so loud) said "No," yet Tony insisted. Evidently, she handed the phone over to the clerk.

Tony asked the clerk why his wife couldn't get a refund, and the clerk repeated the same story about only having $40 available in the cash drawer. Then Tony asked for the manager's name, then the district manager's name, and finally the regional manager's name, threatening the poor clerk that he would call them all after he got off the phone.

The clerk informed Tony that he could issue the refund later in the day after he had more customers to build up his cash, and Tony replied that he would call back every fifteen minutes until his wife got her money. Tony threw his phone across the floor and walked toward me, beet red, steam emitting from his ears. He knew that I had heard the entire conversation. I tried to calm him down.

"Just call the store back and tell the clerk to use the money stored in the safe's change fund," I gently recommended. When Tony followed my advice, the clerk stated that he was already calling the manager to see if he could get the money from the safe for the refund. Tony called back three minutes later (an eternity for him), and the clerk said his manager had permitted him to do just that.

The moral of the story is that this simple solution of going to the safe should have been part of the sales clerk's What-If Arsenal from the get-go—whether the manager was present or not. Giving Lisa her money would have prevented that heated phone call to Tony in the first place.

You see, you can't always predict when your cash register is going to be short, just like gas station attendants can't predict when their supply of gas will run short. When fastballs of everyday life are thrown at you and your organization, you need to have a strategy for hitting homeruns in unstable conditions. It's called life, and the What-If Arsenal is not only a strategy businesses should have, but families, firms, sports teams, governments—you name the organization—should have, too.

The What-If Arsenal would have made Tony and Lisa satisfied and repeat customers. It would have empowered the employee to instantly solve the customer's problem—which is what Fresh Customer Service is all about—and it would have allowed the clerk to focus on providing a World-Class experience to the other customers, who I am sure were thinking to themselves, "Wow, I hope I never have a problem and have to go through what these poor people are going through," while they were likely being ignored on the sidelines as this heated phone match was taking place.

It would have also alleviated the undue stress and brutal feedback that Tony and Lisa were dishing out to the Frontline Employee. Do you really think any employee wants to be subjected to this type of behavior? I would say with confidence they don't. So set them up to succeed personally and professionally.

Fresh Entrée:
Stock Your Arsenal to Clean Up Customer Issues

Not providing employees with a What-If Arsenal is like telling a construction worker to go and build the best house he can, but not giving him a hammer, nails, or a blueprint with which to build it. The What-If Arsenal equips the Frontline Employee with a powerful toolset that will enable him to Make-It-Right-Now for the customer.

Accenture performed its second annual survey of more than 2,000 U.S. and UK consumers in 2006. The survey revealed that more than half (52 percent) of the respondents stated that poor service led them to change service providers in at least one industry in the past year.

Furthermore, The White House Office of Consumer Affairs commissioned a report called the TARP study. The report revealed the following facts about unhappy customers:

- 96 percent of dissatisfied customers do not complain directly.
- 90 percent will not return.
- One unhappy customer will tell nine others.
- 13 percent will tell at least 20 other people.

These statistics are extremely alarming for two reasons: Firstly, the majority of customers will not give you the second opportunity to make it right; and secondly, the unsatisfied customers will share their negative experiences with friends, neighbors, and family. All this data solidifies my belief that delivering a World-Class customer service experience is the single most important aspect of developing and sustaining a healthy business.

In an article titled *Tips for Curing Bad Customer Service* on the Customer Service Manager (CSM) Group website, Art Waller, regional department head for Utah State University, said, "It takes 12 positive service incidents to make up for one negative incident." He continues to say, "Seven out of ten complaining customers will do business with you again if you resolve the complaint in their favor. If you resolve it on the spot, 95 percent will do business with you again."

Thus, it is imperative that we arm our Frontline Employees with tools that can be instantly used to resolve the customer's problem so that they can produce a World-Class customer service experience all the time. The What-If Arsenal is the best strategy, in combination with the others I talk about in this book, to accomplish customer retention.

But here's a tip. We need to be careful not to dictate the contents of the What-If Arsenal toolbox. Filling it with techniques that we think are appropriate for the Frontline Employee while sidelining what the Frontline Employee believes is right will not work.

Instead, we should give Frontline Employees the opportunity to brainstorm their own ideas for filling the toolbox. Subsequently, the role of management will become one of helping Frontline Employees to implement and execute these techniques. Bestowing this level of ownership on the Frontline Employee will foster sincerity, excitement, and empowerment. Not bestowing this ownership sends the message to employees that this is just another corporate bully program being forced on them, whether they like it or not.

There is a great possibility that a company's current policies, procedures, and standards of ethics were not written in consultation with the Frontline Employees. If this is the case, there is a real chance that some of the tools, techniques, and practices that the Frontline Employees suggest could be misaligned with current protocol.

The litmus test should be whether the employees' suggestions are ethical. If they are, they should be implemented. It all comes down to one element: **a World-Class customer service experience** that will grow and sustain your business.

The What-If Arsenal should be a published document that is taught during new hire training, refresher courses, and ongoing training. This document should also be posted in the operations area to serve as a reminder to all Frontline Employees.

A reminder like this is especially important because traditional customer service training has become more and more like learning mathematics than actually teaching and promoting practical thinking. Countless businesses and organizations expend large amounts of capital into fruitless customer service training programs. The new hire is taught theory, statistics, and protocol, and told to read a 10-inch policy and procedures manual.

Yet these programs often fail because they don't focus on teaching and showing customer service-centered behavior, nor do they equip Frontline Employees with a diverse set of tools to deal with everyday problems.

Rarely is the idea of thinking on your feet, *savoir faire*, and empathy instilled in new hires. Rather, theories and stats, along with the hundreds of policies and procedures that if broken could result in getting fired, are ingrained in their minds.

Though these theories, policies, procedures, and statistics are important, do they teach any practical skills? No. They focus on and emphasize numbers and what you can't do, while providing few concrete solutions to how to effectively and efficiently execute the main function of the job, which is delivering a high level of customer service. The What-If Arsenal is about pairing real-world customer problems with real-world solutions that employees know by heart and can use with ease and finesse when they need to transform a bad customer service experience into a good one.

Here is an example of how one retailer discovered a gap in its customer service policy and successfully closed it by implementing a What-if Arsenal. I once consulted at an organization training and mentoring new frontline managers. They came in with a good understanding of how to run operations and perform the technical aspects of the job, but they got hung up on the customer service issue.

There was no process in place for resolving customer problems or rectifying a poor customer experience. One day a manager named Bernadette called me in a panic. A customer had spilled a chemical present at the operation on what she termed a "very expensive" leather coat!

Bernadette had been there seven months and she had gone through the customer service binders at the station, but none of them indicated what to do in an unusual situation like this. She then called the corporate 1-800 help number, but got no answer there, either. During all this time, the chemical was still seeping into the customer's coat, causing more damage.

Not knowing what else to do, Bernadette told the customer to go home and return the next day at 9:00 AM, when the operations manager would be present. The customer was not happy with this resolution for two reasons: She had no coat to wear home, and she could see the chemical causing damage to her leather coat. The customer returned the next day and the coat had blotches of discoloration and emitted a strong odor; basically it had been rendered unusable.

I decided to put a manual together of real experiences like Bernadette's with step-by-step processes to resolve them. In the case of a customer spilling a chemical on a coat, the first step was to have the customer take the coat off for safety reasons. Then the manager would offer to take the coat to the dry cleaners for them and also give them money to purchase a coat to wear in the meantime. In Bernadette's case, her unit was located in New York City, where you don't want to be caught without a coat, especially in mid-November!

On a monthly basis, the management team would get together and share the best practices and the most efficient ways of dealing with customer problems. These solutions and step-by-step processes were added to the binder and a newly developed online guide, called "The Survival Guide," that could be retrieved on the company's intranet.

As a result of these findings, the company decided to review this binder and online document during the first few days of training that frontline managers went through. Previously, managers at this organization had spent hours calling colleagues or anyone else who would pick up the phone in search of advice and the proper process for dealing with various customer service problems. With this fresh tool, they were able to quickly solve many customer problems and move on with their business. The customers were happy and the managers were able to be more productive.

LEAP   Forward in Your Customer Service

Prior to teaching employees the What-If Arsenal, show Frontline Employees how to **LEAP** and quickly turn a customer complaint into a World-Class customer service experience. What is **LEAP,** you ask? A simple, four-step process that can make all the difference between average customer service and World-Class customer service. **LEAP** means:

***L**isten intently with a laser focus on the customer:
  • This exudes a sense of being heard to the customer.
  • And shows that the Frontline Employee cares.

***E**mpathize with the customer:
  • This shows the customer that the Frontline Employee understands the problem.
  • And signals that the Frontline Employee will likely make an attempt to solve the problem.

***A**sk, "What can I do to make you happy?"
  • This puts the power in the customer's hands.
  • And gives the Frontline Employee an opportunity to mentally review if he or she has something in the What-If Arsenal that will make the customer happy.

***P**romise to work to resolve the problem to the best of your ability:
  • This helps the customer understand that action will be

regarded with wholehearted dedication.

- It also gives the Frontline Employees the opportunity to have honest dialogue concerning what problems they can and can't solve personally, but for which they are committed to taking responsibility. It ensures that the problems will be resolved when the person with the appropriate level of authority is made aware of it.

Instilling the LEAP philosophy into all your Frontline Employees is one step (actually, the sixth of nine steps), in fully implementing a What-If Arsenal in your organization. Training your Frontline Employees is the seventh step. All nine steps follow:

1. Find out from the Frontline Employees what would enable them to better solve customer problems.

2. Ask employees for their favorite problem-solving strategies. Document them.

3. Devise a list of solutions that will go into the What-If Arsenal.

4. Check this list against your policy, procedures, and ethics to ensure alignment. Don't be afraid to challenge your existing policies if a World-Class customer service experience is being impeded.

5. Publish the What-If Arsenal.

6. Teach Frontline Employees how to LEAP and quickly turn a customer's complaint into a World-Class customer

service experience.

7. Provide fresh and fun training for your What-If Arsenal.

8. Constantly review the What-If Arsenal to ensure fresh-ness and its alignment with the changing environment.

9. Don't be afraid to add or delete from the What-If Arsenal. Keep it fresh!

The customer shouldn't have to donate his or her precious and rare time to your business because of ill-equipped and powerless employees. I'll bet you can think of many instanc-es when a What-If Arsenal would have helped a Frontline Employee provide you with a World-Class customer service experience and prevented you from donating your personal time (due to the extended wait) to the company.

The world is constantly changing and so are the needs, wants, and desires of our customers and Frontline Employ-ees. To that end, we must keep the What-If Arsenal fresh and be ready to respond to these changes in a proactive, ver-sus a reactive, way. We should continue to poll our Frontline Employees for fresh tools, practices, and resources to feed and nourish the What-If Arsenal often.

If it helps, think of the Frontline Employee as the skilled artist who can take the provided canvas, paint brushes, and colors to create a World-Class customer service experience masterpiece for which customers will pay top dollar. Not only will they pay top dollar for this experience, it will also be framed and etched into their minds to be shared with friends, colleagues, and even strangers.

Exercise in Creating a Winning Training Agenda

So here's the scenario: you have a group of new employees in the organization. You want to ensure that they understand what is meant by World-Class customer service and the What-If Arsenal. Below is a framework to help you create a training session with a new employee. Here are four items that should be the core of your agenda:

• Why is providing a World-Class customer service experience important?

• Why types of behaviors are needed to deliver a World-Class customer service experience?

• What is the What-if-Arsenal? (Be sure to let them know that the What-If-Arsenal is comprised of suggestions from Frontline Employees just like them.)

• Brainstorm for fresh ideas. (Look for additions to the What-If Arsenal.)

Write a list of solutions that will go in the What-If Arsenal. In the left-hand column, write the problems the employees discussed in the previous exercise. In the right hand column, write about the best practice solutions to these problems. Please see the example on the following page, taken from an

Current Problems	Solutions
Customers are always complaining that we don't have their car ready by the promised delivery time. A customer just said to me on Friday, "You guys never have my car ready by the promised time. I dropped my car off at 8:00 AM, and you told me that it would be ready at noon. I rushed over here, and it's not ready."	Suggested responses for the Frontline Employee: "I apologize that we weren't able to meet your expectations. Please tell me what we can do to make you happy and exceed your expectations." **Or** "Can we offer you a free car wash for your extended wait? Again, I apologize for us not having your car ready." **Or** The management team should implement a policy to deliver on the promise made to the customer. A check should be made by the manager within one hour of the promised delivery time. If additional time is required, the manager should contact the customer and make them aware of the new delivery time.

auto dealership.

So work with your "Picassos"—the Frontline Employees—to develop a robust canvas, a set of strong reliable tools, and let them help pick out the fresh colors to be used to paint, frame, and present to the customers the masterpiece that is Fresh Customer Service. Go ahead, unleash the Picassos and watch the results unfold.

Temperature Check

Now that you have all the ingredients to create a tasty What-If Arsenal, it's time to get in the kitchen and start cooking! Once you think you have the recipe down pat, take some time to check the temperature.

1. Call your office or place of business and pose a very common customer problem to the person who answers the phone. What did you think of the response?

2. Are your customers receiving the same level of response to their problem/opportunity when the manager is away?

3. Pose a What-If situation to one of the newest Frontline Employees. Is he prepared to provide an instant solution or does he look dazed, confused, or clueless?

4. When was the last time your Frontline Employees were provided with new solutions to new customer problems?

5. Are your Frontline Employees still solving problems with solutions that are no longer satisfying the customer's changing needs?

6. Call or visit your competitor and see how they solve the same problem. Are they better at instantly solving the problem than your organization?

6.5. Interview three of your Frontline Employees. Ask if they feel empowered and equipped with the necessary solutions to instantly solve their customers' problems.

As a general guideline, you should be extremely satisfied with the response you get to any customer problems you pose your own business, and you should feel confident that you are doing a better job than your competitors at handling similar customer problems. Your Frontline Employees should be regularly receiving updates to their What-If Arsenal that reflect changing customer tastes and needs, and Frontline Employees should have the empowerment and capability to instantly solve customer problems, whether a manager is present or not.

When you can honestly say that your organization has met all these conditions, then you have a well-done What-If Arsenal ready to serve to Frontline Employees and customers alike!

What's your Temperature? The What-If Arsenal

Temperature	Correct Response Rate	Explanation
Rare	0 correct Temperature Check responses	A customer with a problem had better pray an equipped and empowered manager is close by, because otherwise they're out of luck!
Medium Rare	1-2 correct Temperature Check responses	Frontline Employees have limited capabilities to resolve customer issues, but the results probably aren't very satisfactory for anyone involved.
Medium	3-4 correct Temperature Check responses	Frontline Employees have a sincere desire to resolve customer issues and do the best they can, but your competitor is probably doing it better.
Medium Well	5-6 correct Temperature Check responses	Frontline Employees are empowered to resolve customer issues and have the authority and confidence to do so instantly. But their methods may be a little out of date, or some situations may still throw them for a loop.
Well Done	**6.5 correct Temperature Check responses**	A customer problem is no problem for your Frontline Employees, who can quickly resolve virtually any situation that arises. Even if they can't deal with a problem on their own, they know how to efficiently move through the proper channels to provide a fresh resolution.

*Keep checking the temperature to make sure you get to Well Done and stay there

Fresh Technologies

Advances in the capabilities of business intelligence (BI) systems, which can crunch terabytes of data with relative ease, can be put to use to help create and maintain your What-If Arsenal. Massive data warehousing/mining platforms are capable of storing, filtering, and processing trading data collected and transmitted via company intranet to identify important facts and trends, such as customer complaints and issues.

By employing such a BI system, you can stay on top of trends in customer service problems as they develop, and receive assistance in devising effective, convenient solutions that will make both your customers and your Frontline Employees happy. It is often said that "knowledge is power." BI systems enable an organization to extract knowledge it never even realized it possessed, and the results are definitely empowering!

Take Out

1. Involve Frontline Employees in developing your What-If Arsenal from the beginning. They are the ones who will

observe the customer complaints and issues that need to be addressed first-hand, and they have the direct experience and knowledge to resolve them. Always keep the needs of Frontline Employees in mind when devising resolutions to customer issues.

2. After collecting data for your What-If Arsenal, don't sit on it or bury it in rarely-used and hard-to-understand corporate documents. Actively show your Frontline Employees how to utilize the What-If Arsenal in their daily interactions with customers, and train them how to properly follow What-If Arsenal procedures.

3. Keep the What-If Arsenal fresh. A resolution that worked five years ago may not work today, and a problem that was common five years ago may not exist today. Conversely, new problems will constantly arise, and they will require new solutions. Keep avenues of communication between the frontline and the corporate office wide open. As mentioned above, the Frontline Employees are the first ones to experience customer issues, and they often have the best insight on how to resolve them.

Fresh Step ⑤
Bubble-Up Innovation

 **Fresh Appetizer:**
Are We Having Fun Yet?

In my experience, the most relevant, effective, and useful solutions to improving any aspect of an organization have come from those who have face-to-face roles with customers. This phenomenon is called **Bubble-Up Innovation**—fresh ideas and contributions from Frontline Employees on how everyone can do things better. When Bubble-Up Innovation is encouraged, appreciated, and enacted, it can transform a good organization into a great organization.

When I want to encourage innovation and gain solutions to problems facing the business, I schedule a "Bubble-Up Innovation Fun Day." I create an off-site environment that promotes innovation, represents the brand and desired customer experience, and, above all, is comfortable and stimulating for the Frontline Employee.

I don't create just any ordinary brainstorming day. You won't find me bringing employees into a stale meeting room containing a plain boardroom table, fluorescent lights, hard-backed chairs, and flip charts galore. This, to me, is uninspiring and just begs for an unproductive "sleeper" meeting. I foster an unconventional environment, which I believe to be one of the keys to encouraging the kind of feedback that will spark innovation.

I hold my Innovation Fun Days in a room that's transformed to resemble a slightly less pastel "Pee Wee's Playhouse." I make sure bean bags, cushy reclining chairs, and a couch replace stiff chairs. I pop in a CD of jazzy background music, toss in some stress balls and trinkets, and never forget to pick up some fresh flowers. Fresh air, good ventilation, and a comfortable temperature helps.

Because I know that the way to people's hearts is through their stomachs, I make sure to stock the Fun Day atmosphere with plenty of snacks (and if your company produces or sells food, make sure those are prominently featured among the treats you offer at your Fun Day). When employees walk in, they will instantly feel excited, valued, creative, gung-ho and ready to work.

Fresh Entrée:
Buon Appetito Café, Part 2 and How Did Starbucks Get So Darned Successful?

I brought a similar Fun Day to the previously mentioned Buon Appetito Café, even though this was above and beyond what I was actually hired to do. In addition to having problems with its new gourmet sandwiches not meeting customer expectations, Buon Appetito Café was suffering from the unpleasant effects of slow service caused by the introduction of the new gourmet sandwiches.

Customers had been slowly filing out and not visiting Buon Appetito Café ever since they had introduced those new gourmet sandwiches, which were complex to execute. Several steps were involved in their preparation and actual assembly. After about two months of the new sandwich offer, Buon Appetito's leadership hired mystery shoppers to evaluate the business. The new sandwiches scored about average in taste (by this point, customers had become more familiar with the ingredients and were made aware that they could alter the sandwiches' ingredients), freshness, and price. So why weren't loyal customers returning anymore?

Because the average wait time for a sandwich had now become greater than eight minutes. The company made a new goal to get it down to three minutes—the extended wait time was hurting business and threatening future success of the operation. But how were they going to reduce the gourmet sandwich-making time by 60 percent?

I initiated a casual conversation with the frontline team from a Buon Appetito branch about the problems with their speed of service (or lack thereof). The environment in which we conducted this dialogue was casual, comfortable, and very open, and I made particular effort to make sure everyone was heard.

About forty-five minutes into the meeting, an employee in her mid-twenties named Beverly said, "You know, the thing that takes a lot of our time is correcting the mistakes that we make when we put the wrong sauce on the customer's sandwich. Once we put the wrong sauce on the bread, we have to throw it away and start over."

I looked around the room and every head began to nod. I probed a little deeper, and another employee explained that the twelve different sauces were all in clear plastic bottles and stored in a deep pan where you couldn't see the label.

A sandwich-maker named Dan said, "We just look at the top of the bottle and think that we are picking up the right sauce. In an effort to make the sandwich quickly, we squirt the sauce on the bread without really looking down. As we are moving to the next step, we realize that we put the wrong sauce on the bread. For example, we have three different kinds of mustard, and they are all yellow, so oftentimes we pick up the wrong kind of mustard, too."

Everyone looked at each other in agreement.

We went on with this discussion for about twenty more minutes. One employee, a big-boned guy named Phil, said, "I have an idea—why don't we put the name of the sauce on the top of the bottle, so that we can readily see it?"

The group became exuberant and started clapping. It may have been one small step for the employees, but it was a giant leap for Buon Appetito. The staff was experiencing a collective breakthrough; they were putting their heads together to solve a problem. Soon afterward, we found a vendor that could produce a ring label that would fit over the top of the sauce bottle.

One month later, the staff decreased its wait time by two minutes and reduced waste by 29 percent. While room for improvement certainly still existed, Buon Appetito Café was on its way to offering a World-Class customer service experience.

Creating an open, relaxed, and off-work-hour environment for Bubble-Up Innovation is crucial because it stimulates creative suggestions from the Frontline Employees about the best ways to improve the operation. I emphasize this because all too often, when we want to get feedback from our Frontline Employees, we walk up to them while they are performing their duties and ask, "What can we do to improve?"

This approach catches them off-guard when their mind is focused on the immediate needs of serving the customer. And the majority of the time, employees will not open up under these circumstances because they are uncomfortable with such a tactless approach.

One of the biggest mistruths I find myself correcting in friends and colleagues is that innovation and openness to new (or "wild") ideas has always been present at large, successful companies—and it's the smaller-scale and less successful companies that need to practice innovation. Some will just agree in order to spare themselves my lecture on the need for all companies to foster and support innovation among Frontline Employees.

But let me highlight what one of my most admired leaders, Howard Schultz, Chairman and Chief Global Strategist of Starbucks Corporation, writes about in his book, *Pour Your Heart Into It: How Starbucks Built a Company One Cup at a Time.*

Schultz says that many entrepreneurs fall into the same trap: "They are so captivated by their own vision that when an employee comes up with an idea, especially one that doesn't seem to fit the original vision, they are tempted to quash it."

Schultz remembers that he nearly did the same for one of Starbucks' most successful products, the frothy blend of ice, roasted coffee and milk called the Frappuccino. He says that many people working in his Southern California stores had repeatedly requested that Starbucks sell some type of chilled, blended beverage.

But because the leadership didn't believe the frappe-like treat to be a bona-fide coffee drink, they refused to budge. Schultz says he especially resisted the idea. "It seemed to dilute the integrity of what we stood for and sounded more like a fast-food shake than something a true coffee lover would enjoy," he writes.

After some persistence and the Frontline Employees' reworking of the recipe, Schultz approved the drink. In the first full year on the national market, which was in 1996, he writes that Starbucks sold $52 million worth of Frappuccinos, which represented 7 percent of their total revenues. "That's 52 million (dollars) we would not have registered had we not listened to our partners in California," says Schultz.

If Schultz's experience at Starbucks does not prove my theory that Frontline Employees know the business as well, if not better, than leadership, I don't know what does. Being privy to changing customer needs, as well as witnessing the struggles and stumbles of the customers long before anyone else ever notices, makes Frontline Employees the perfect World-Class customer service architects.

Therefore, we should willingly and unselfishly give Frontline Employees the space, approval, and support to be innovative. This will ignite in the Frontline Employees not only a passion for the experience that he can offer the customers, but for the business as a whole. And believe it or not, a passionate employee's energy and enthusiasm rubs off on the customer—and they in turn become passionate about your business and scream your praises to others.

I will tell you a quick story about how I myself became converted to this theory. I was in the Atlanta Hartsfield Airport about five years ago. I noticed a man standing next to me clutching a cup of Starbucks coffee and sipping it as if he were sipping on a Lafite-Rothschild Bordeaux wine (disguised in a paper cup). After a few minutes he took the liberty of asking me if I had ever tried Starbucks' Caramel Macchiato.

"I don't see why anyone would pay five bucks for a cup of coffee," I replied. His eyes widened and a smile appeared instantly on his face. Had I known then what I know now, I wouldn't have opened this can of worms.

For the next ten minutes he told me about how it's more than just a cup of coffee—it's the experience. "The barista at the Starbucks near my work knows my name, and he knows how I like my Caramel Macchiato," this coffee junkie said. "The employees are so nice every time I go in!"

As if his exclamations weren't convincing enough, he proceeded to tell me how I should order the Caramel Macchiato when *I* go to Starbucks. He sounded more like a baking recipe than someone who was supposedly ordering a coffee. And guess what? He delivered this whole conversation with a degree of passion that only a CEO or a shareholder who had just had their dividends tripled could have done. I asked him if he was either and he told me he was merely a loyal fan.

By the time two weeks had passed, that Carmel Macchiato-crazed lunatic had me converted! And to this day, I enjoy a triple grande with whipped Caramel Macchiato three times a week (at least)… all thanks to that passionate customer I met in the Atlanta airport!

Why is Bubble-Up Innovation so important?
Frontline Employees have viewpoints and experiences that only they can articulate. Bubble-Up Innovation is the best way to harness and implement this feedback. Their sugges-

tions will make your organization stand out from competition, and enhance the bottom line. So make a concerted effort to tap into this innovation and encourage Frontline Employees to share their ideas.

The following are tips to create structures and mechanisms that support and sustain innovation:

- Place a tape recorder in the Bubble-Up "zone" where employees can record their ideas. Employees are more likely to give you ideas if they don't have to spend a lot of time writing them down.

- Rewards and recognition. You want to encourage and reward innovative behaviors. Gift certificates, prepaid cash cards, free dinner, movie tickets, and spot bonuses (instant cash recognition) are all good incentives.

- Provide a simple form like the one on the next page that employees can fill out. While many people are more likely to give you ideas off the cuff verbally, some employees feel more comfortable writing their ideas on paper. This is a way to encourage that segment of the population.

I took a customer's lemons and made lemonade out of them...and they didn't even complain!

If I tell you how I did it, do you promise to keep making lemonade?

OK, here is what I did:

CUSTOMER PROBLEM: _____

_____

HOW DID I SOLVE THE PROBLEM? _____

_____

HOW DID THEY FEEL IN THE END? _____

_____

EMPLOYEE NAME: _____

_____

DATE: _____

Temperature Check

OK, so you're whipping up a fresh batch of Bubble Up Information. Is it ready to eat, or is it still rare and undercooked? Review the following checklist to find out.

1. If an employee has an idea, how does it reach the proper person for examination?

2. Is there a process in place to encourage innovation?

3. What resources are dedicated each year to encourage,

extract, and execute ideas that are generated by the Frontline Employees?

4. What could prevent your organization from implementing Bubble-Up Innovation?

5. Do you personally have an idea or innovation that could help the process, but have not yet shared it?

6. Does your current office setting promote or stifle creativity and innovation?

6.5. Starbucks earned an extra $52 million dollars by finally allowing creativity and innovation to flow. How much could your organization earn by doing the same?

Many of these questions are open-ended, but keep in mind that you must have a process in place to encourage innovation, and your office setting needs to promote creativity and innovation. You don't want to limit employee creativity to the confines of the annual Fun Day. It should be relatively easy for any employee to get an idea to the proper person for examination. This includes the executives, the leadership team, and any other decision-makers. Are you sitting on an innovative idea? Shame on you!

Once you have a smooth flow of creativity and innovation that runs from the frontline through the corporate headquarters straight to the boardroom, you will have a well-done Bubble Up Innovation process. To measure your progress with the Temperature Check chart, consider how many of your responses give you an honest feeling that you are successfully implementing and maintaining Bubble-Up Innovation at your organization. *Bon appetit!*

What's your Temperature? Bubble-Up Innovation

Temperature	Correct Response Rate	Explanation
Rare	0 correct Temperature Check responses	Innovation? That's something which comes out of closed-door board meetings and executive retreats!
Medium Rare	1-2 correct Temperature Check responses	There may be an annual "Fun Day" or employee suggestion box, but nobody really does much with the suggestions.
Medium	3-4 correct Temperature Check responses	Innovative ideas gathered from annual events or employee suggestions are reviewed and occasionally acted upon, but it's not a day-to-day effort.
Medium Well	5-6 correct Temperature Check responses	Every employee, from the front line to the back office, operates in an environment that actively encourages innovation and creativity. All suggestions are given their due. But somehow, it doesn't translate to any significant gains in profits or productivity.
Well Done	**6.5 correct Temperature Check responses**	Your organization is a streamlined innovation engine. Nobody would even consider sitting on an idea they thought might help the company's performance and improve the customer experience. And the bean counters are pretty happy with the results, too!

*Keep checking the temperature to make sure you get to Well Done and stay there

Fresh Technologies

Bubble Up Innovation is a bit more of a low-tech process than many of the other Fresh Steps reviewed in this book, but that doesn't mean technology can't still play a key role in helping to get ideas from the frontline to the back office, where they're desperately needed! Here are a few quick technology tips:

- Offer employees an email address where they can send their ideas. Frontline Employees are more computer savvy than generations past. Many of them prefer using email as a method of communication. The process should be simple, easy to remember, and take very little time to complete. Here's an example of an email address they might use: Gotidea@yourcompany.com.

- Start an internal blog. Blogs are a great way to have an open electronic dialogue. This provides thousands of people in the organization the opportunity to join in and contribute to one huge dialogue. They can actually be quite informative and fun; check out mine at www.the-michaeldbrown.com.

- Provide a fax number for employees to fax in their ideas. A fax number is just another way to encourage participation for employees who don't have access to the Internet or just feel more comfortable faxing. Here's an example of a possible fax number: 1-800-Got-Idea.

• Create site-level exposure. All that high-falutin' technology won't do you much good if nobody can see the results! Use an employee bulletin board and/or company newsletter/communication notes to display all the ideas that have come from the website, tape recorder, written ideas, the fax number, etc. The ideas should be placed on the employee bulletin board for recognition and the sharing of winning practices.

Take Out

1. Actively engage Frontline Employees in all Bubble-Up Innovation activities. Bubble-Up Innovation is not about employees gathering to hear a management presentation on how to more creatively approach their jobs. As the name implies, it is about taking innovation from the frontline of the organization and distributing it upward until it reaches the decision-makers.

2. Foster innovation on a day-to-day basis, not just during an annual or semi-annual special event. Give Frontline Employees the space and time needed to encourage innovative thoughts, ideas, and actions. Don't forget to use the vehicles discussed in Chapter 5 as mechanisms for Frontline Employees to channel up the innovative ideas. Properly applied, Bubble-Up Innovation is an everyday

process that can occur randomly at any given time. It needs to be free-form and unrestrained.

3. Help encourage employees to share their innovative ideas by providing rewards and recognition for doing so. Your rewards and recognition program can be multi-faceted to provide different incentives for different levels of innovation. For example, an employee who makes a suggestion that does not wind up getting implemented may be entered in a monthly drawing to receive a gift certificate to a local restaurant, while an employee who makes a suggestion that is used with positive results may receive extra paid vacation time or a cash bonus.

Fresh Step 6
Relentless Focus

Fresh Appetizer: Everybody's Working
on the Weekend (or Should Be)

For some reason I think I have "tell me about your company" written on my forehead. Soon after I meet people and tell them what I do for a living, they feel compelled to pour their souls out to me about their jobs or businesses. I'm not sure if it's a method of crying out for help or if my demeanor is too serious for talk about the weather or what one ate for lunch. Be that as it may, I am glad people feel comfortable telling me their stories.

Some time ago, I was working out in the gym alongside a guy who appeared to be in the same predicament as I. Namely, I was deciding whether to just stare at the weights and hope that they lifted themselves out of the cradle, pick up the weights and start working out, or go to the store and have a low-fat doughnut.

This guy, who was named Kelvin, seemed to be in his mid-twenties. After finally picking up the weights and completing a few sets, Kelvin started to ask the gym ego question, "How much can you lift?"

Not your average gym rat, my reply was: "So where do you work?"

Kelvin told me he worked at a very well-known home do-it-yourself (DIY) store that I'll call "House Headquarters." I didn't hesitate to mention to Kelvin that I thought House Headquarters' customer service had gone downhill in recent years and their chief competitor had become much better at customer service.

"I agree, our customer service is shabby," Kelvin said, exhaling mightily while 75-pound dumbbells slammed to the gym's cushioned floor. "I'll tell you a story.

"I was recently working with a customer who became extremely upset with us. This customer purchased a brand name, side-by-side, built-in refrigerator for almost $8,000. Once it was delivered, he called back, stating that the install had a gap in between the walls and the refrigerator of about three inches, whereas the model in the store was flush together. He was right. This refrigerator has a true built-in appearance and looks very flush with the wall in the store. I told him I'd look into it.

"So I called the regional installation supervisor, and he said he would check out the situation," Kelvin said, his arms shaking from the heavy dumbbell. (There goes my gym ego again.) "You know, we always have problems and complaints with this installer, but we still have to use them because they're our national contractor. I don't know what's going to happen with this customer, but I feel really badly for him.

"I sent the installer back out on Saturday," Kelvin continued. "But I won't be able to get back with the customer until Monday because I have to see what the regional installation supervisor, who doesn't work on weekends, says. The customer sent me pictures of the install, and it is really bad. I just don't know why we keep using this installer. We've all gotten complaints about this particular installation company."

The lesson here: The entire organization needs to be focused on providing a World-Class customer service experience. I would think that someone should have been in contact with this customer throughout the weekend to ensure that his problem was solved. House Headquarters likely does a large chunk of their business on the weekend, as this is when people are doing home projects. This type of weekend service is even more important for a customer who has just paid the company a lot of money.

The quicker you solve the problem, the greater the opportunity for making the customer happy and keeping him or her coming back. If the frontline is not empowered or it does not have immediate access to someone who is empowered (as in Kelvin's case) to provide an instant solution to the problem, the problem will remain with the customer longer and fester into something greater and cause him or her to be even more dissatisfied with the experience.

Question: Is this just an isolated incident for House Headquarters, or is my view and the employee's view true, that their customer service is substandard? Is it really impossible for Kelvin or his colleagues to provide a good customer experience with an incompetent contractor? A review by the leadership team is in order.

Kelvin seems to have been focused on delivering a good customer experience—his heart was indeed as big as the biceps that we both aspired to have after working out (yes, I am still aspiring as I sit here writing). However, the weekend unavailability of the regional installation supervisor made it impossible to deliver a World-Class customer service experience.

The regional installation supervisor's availability—or a designee's—would have provided Kelvin with the important missing link needed to deliver an instant solution to the customer's problem (remember this is the foundation of Fresh Customer Service—solving the problem *now*, making it right now for the customer).

In addition, the person in charge of the independent contractors appears to have not responded to the negative feedback voiced by both customers and Frontline Employees. After all, it seems that this shoddy contractor is the root cause of current and previous problems.

Relentless Focus is about a steady, persistent, unyielding, and committed focus on providing a World-Class customer service experience 24 hours a day, seven days a week by everyone in the organization. This focus doesn't take a break or go on vacation and is always present.

Many organizations are good at "kick-off celebrations." Most customer service programs start off with a bang, with everyone being committed and poised to make them happen. But as the strategies start changing, new leaders come in, employees become disinterested, and the focus shifts to something else, the initial great customer service program is tossed aside like a child's old favorite toy.

Relentless Focus forces the organization to make an ongoing investment in providing a World-Class customer service experience by embedding it into the core business model. Every program, strategy, and initiative has an automatic space carved out for providing a World-Class customer service experience. Not providing this focus destroys the foundation of the operation and the goal of providing a great customer experience.

Because a World-Class customer service experience is the foundation of any successful operation, Relentless Focus on customer service predetermines the ultimate success of any operation. If the focus on customer service is lost, then employees begin to believe that the organization isn't really committed to its customer service goals or any of its other programs, initiatives, or strategies.

Fresh Entrée: Avoiding Silos and Mystery Shopping your Way to Success

How can you achieve Relentless Focus? Start by following these helpful hints:

1. Post a plain and a simple statement on the communal cork board (or employee blog, etc.) affirming the organization's commitment to providing a World-Class customer service experience.

2. Gain a buy-in from every person and facet of the organization so that everyone knows they are accountable for providing a World-Class customer service experience 100 percent of the time.

3. Train all employees on the best ways to maintain this focus while executing any task.

4. New generations will enter the workplace, customer demands will change, and the competitive landscape will morph. It behooves the organization to constantly review the customer experience to ensure that it is competitive and still executable by the employees.

5. Make the World-Class customer experience part of the corporate culture, goals, and strategies. Don't turn it into some kind of "program of the month" that is forgotten the day the calendar changes over to the first of the next month.

While you are implementing Relentless Focus throughout your organization, remember this critical fact: **It is impossible to deliver a World-Class customer service experience if people of the organization are working in "silos," a concept synonymous with barriers that separate work teams, departments, and divisions.**

Silos cause people who work for the same employer to compete against one another, often because a clear directive or strategy is not communicated. In silo-driven organizations, managers, department heads, and program managers care a great deal about their own little departments but are oblivious (sometimes purposefully) to other priorities that affect the greater good of the company as a whole. Unfortunately, these ignored priorities can include the most important one of all, providing a World-Class customer service experience.

The leadership team needs to clearly and explicitly communicate to every member of the organization that providing a World-Class customer service experience through Fresh Customer Service is the foundation of the business and is the responsibility of every member. It unequivocally comes before any silo competition.

The leadership team should understand that a mere statement of the need to provide a World-Class customer service experience will not guarantee success, especially if a silo mentality exists. The only way to successfully achieve outstanding customer service is by getting everyone involved and backing it wholeheartedly. Members of the workforce should exit their silos and abandon the silo mentality for the good of all the Frontline Employees and customers, and consequently, the bottom line.

One way of gaining team involvement is by finding a way to rally the employees around a common thematic goal. In his recent book, *Silos, Politics, and Turf Wars: A Leadership Fable*

About Destroying the Barriers That Turn Colleagues Into Competitors, management consultant Patrick Lencioni describes a thematic goal as "a single, qualitative focus that is shared by the entire leadership team, and ultimately, by the entire organization."

This drive and rally to move the organization toward a thematic goal of delivering a World-Class customer service experience must be initiated from the very top if it is to gain traction and move forward. This movement should be done quickly and with a sense of urgency. It should be done in the spirit of fun, excitement, and inclusiveness.

People are more likely to embrace change when it's fun. Fear should not be a tactic to get employees to buy into improving customer service. **Humans, as I've said before, are conditioned to run from fear, not embrace it.** The organization must have a laser-sharp focus on creating, delivering, and even exceeding a World-Class customer service experience through Fresh Customer Service.

Additionally, and I am especially speaking to the C-level executives reading this, please do not create or tolerate a distance between the corporate office structure and the Frontline Employees. The more disconnect that is allowed, the more fresh greenbacks it will take you to get back to the source of strategy, the source of your solutions, and the foundations of your business.

And yes, it may cost a bit more than a first class international airline ticket to restructure the echelons within your business. If you are insistent that some distance must exist between the upper and lower ranks, make sure it's a Southwest Airlines gap (where you can get connected for $49 minus the frills), rather than a civilian space travel gap (the world's first recorded civilian space tourist, American millionaire Dennis Tito, reportedly paid the Russian space program a cool $20 million for a jaunt to the International Space Station).

Question: Who is accountable for delivering a World-Class customer experience in the following scenario?

I walked into an outlet of a leading health and nutrition store one day and started to browse a little. I asked the cashier if they had any other flavors of a particular protein meal replacement drink. The shelf had about four bottles of a "Mountain Ice" flavor, and the other spots were empty. He walked me to the back of the store and kicked his feet toward some other flavors located in a box underneath a shelf, and then he walked away.

I reached under the shelf and picked up a case. He never came back to help me. Worse yet, I went back to the store three days later, and no one had taken the product from underneath the counter and stocked the shelf.

Who is holding this employee accountable? Who is holding the manager accountable? And who is holding the district manager accountable at this store? Who is responsible for ensuring a positive customer experience?

Answer: A World-Class customer experience doesn't just happen by osmosis. It is the responsibility of each and every member of the organization to uphold and deliver it 365 days a year.

Measure the results

Once a thematic goal of Relentless Focus has been embraced, and Fresh Customer Service is embedded into the culture, strategy, goals, and objectives, then it is time to measure progress and success. The results should be measured both quantitatively and qualitatively.

Quantitative results are "hard" results that can be measured precisely. For example, after successfully performing a Side-By-Side Walking exercise and acting upon the results, you may see a 12 percent increase in bottom-line profits.

In contrast, qualitative results are "soft" results that cannot be summed up in neat facts and figures, but are nonetheless real. For example, as a result of Side-By-Side Walking, Frontline Employee attitudes toward senior management may improve.

Both types of results are extremely important. Before following any of the Fresh Steps in this book you should first figure out what type of quantitative and qualitative results you are seeking.

There are three tools that we can use to measure World-Class customer experience:

I. A mystery shop program that is conducted by an anonymous shopper who shops at the business and then answers a simple set of questions about the operations, promotional offers, and the customer service experienced. The shopping should happen unannounced and be conducted at random times on various days. It will give valuable information about whether Frontline Employees are delivering the expected level of customer service. Some sample questions you could use include:

- How many seconds did it take for the employee to greet you after you entered the location? *(quantitative result)*

- Were you given a pleasant and sincere greeting? *(qualitative result)*

- How long did you wait in line? *(quantitative result)*

- Describe the appearance and cleanliness of the inside and outside of the operation. *(qualitative result)*

Does anybody get it?

After much consideration, I agreed to be a mystery shopper for a national home builder. They wanted to check to see if several of their sales associates were appropriately executing their ideal home-selling experience. So they asked me to visit two of their brand new communities on two different days and evaluate three of their sales associates.

I would venture to say this national home builder was placing a premium on the sales approach, making it so that the sales team truly understood the customer's needs and the goal of combining this with an outstanding selection of homes available for purchase.

I was provided with a list of forty short-answer questions, and several more requiring narrative answers with which I was to evaluate the sales associates. I journeyed out to see the property and evaluate the associates on two different days, Wednesday and Friday.

One associate was a woman in her early fifties who seemed to have been in this business for quite some time. The other was a gentleman in his late thirties who, when he was standing, towered over me like a giant. This guy seemed a little too slick for his own good. The last gentleman I saw on my last day at the more exclusive property was younger and tried to rush things with a hurried demeanor. Nonetheless, I spent some quality time as a potential new homebuyer with all the sales associates.

After I finished my evaluations, my conclusions outlined how at some point, somewhere, on a particular day at a particular time, a particular sales associate failed at the customer service experience. The focus on the customer, which the home builder had prescribed on paper to be the paramount objective, turned out to be totally absent from the frontline experience delivered by each sales associate at each home site.

Furthermore, all three salespeople delivered the frontline experience drastically differently, but none came close to providing the home builder's desired experience. Of the forty questions on my questionnaire, there were twelve "big" questions that were fundamental in creating the customer experience that would ultimately move the potential buyer to a purchasing decision, according to the company. Each sales associate failed in the Relentless Focus aspect. The following are the twelve "big" questions where they fell short:

1. Did the sales associate determine the shopper's irritations, problems, and/or concerns with his current home/community?

2. Did the sales associate ask the shopper how his irritations, problems, and concerns are affecting him?

3. Did the sales associate ask the shopper what would happen if he did not move?

4. Did the sales associate determine the shopper's current purchasing situation?

5. Did the sales associate ask the shopper to describe a "picture" of his new home?

6. Did the sales associate find out how the shopper's "picture of new" compares to his current home?

7. Did the sales associate ask why his "picture of new" is important to him?

8. Did the sales associate determine the shopper's price range for a new home?

9. Did the sales associate discuss home options based on the shopper's indicated needs?

10. Did the sales associate determine the shopper's prioritization of his new home needs?

11. Did the sales associate ask the shopper why he is considering this property?

12. Did the sales associate ask for the sale?

With so much of the customer experience forfeited because of the sales associates' lack of focus on these questions, I'd say there was much room for improvement. Firstly, not everyone in the organization was on the same page—it seemed as if the sales associates did not even know these questions should be an active part of their selling repertoire. Secondly, it almost seemed as if they didn't see the value of the questions in the first place. Or maybe they just didn't start out possessing the capability to deliver the prescribed experience.

If the home builder is truly committed to delivering an ideal customer experience for the good of its customers and its bottom line, senior management needs to focus on the gap between what they expect to be the ideal customer service experience versus what I, the mystery shopper, actually found during my mystery shopping excursions.

This would mean making sure every sales agent not only asks the questions, but respects them as a part of the homebuilder's game plan for creating a World-Class customer service experience. This would also mean the Frontline Employees—the agents—have to understand the value in delivering this precise experience, and also be capable of delivering it.

II. Use the FRESH Smile Program, a program that entails visiting the Frontline operations of the company and observing the employees to see if they are providing a "FRESH Smile." The Frontline Employees who provide a FRESH Smile can be rewarded on the spot via a thank you, the completed smile form (see below), or incentives such as gift cards, movie tickets, and "company bucks."

*FRESH Smile

Fond greeting… Give a warm welcome.

Remember the customer's name or something about his or her needs, wants, and desires.

Exceed his or her expectations and Enjoy the experience with him or her.

Smile and look for opportunities to Supplement his or her experience (e.g. with upselling/cross selling).

Hearty farewell is extended.

And Keep the SMILE!

On the following page is an example of a FRESH Smile form that could be used:

Providing a World-Class customer service experience with a Fresh Smile!

Catch a Fresh Smile!

Fond greeting… Give a warm welcome.

Remember the customer's name or something about her needs, wants, and desires.

Exceed her expectations and **E**njoy the experience with her.

Smile and look for opportunities to **S**upplement her experience (e.g. with upselling/cross- selling).

Hearty farewell is extended.

Keep the SMILE!

Frontline Employee's name: _____

Date: _____

Name (office employee): _____

😊 *Thanks for keeping the experience Fresh!*

III. The Upselling Program can be performed at an operational level or as a corporate-wide program. Either way, it should measure a Frontline Employee's ability to improve the customer experience through providing additional value to the customers via upselling and cross-selling.

A Real-World Example of How Relentless Focus Resolves a Customer Complaint

Below is the transcript of an online chat I actually had with a customer service representative at a well-known discount web retailer I'll call "Surplus Specialists." This conversation went on for thirty-nine minutes. It's a great example of how Relentless Focus works, though we can debate if it should take thirty-nine minutes to do so.

Welcome to Surplus Specialists Customer Service. You are now chatting with Christina.

Christina: Thank you for visiting Surplus Specialists. How may I help you today?

Me: Christina, I have realized that I omitted an item from the order that I placed last night—order #10018314.

Christina: I will certainly help you with that. To help you better, may I have the invoice number?

Me: 28017716.

Christina: For security purposes, may I ask you to verify the name and billing address on your account?

Me: Michael Brown
1234 Main Street
Pleasant, CA 91785

Christina: Thank you for verifying the name and billing address. May I place you on hold for a minute or two while I research this for you?

Me: Yes.

Christina: Thank you for staying online. I am sorry to say that the order has already been processed and sent to the warehouse. You cannot add the catalog number 10018314 along with this order. However, you can order once more for this item.

Me: I want to take advantage of my 10 percent discount and the $2.95 shipping.

Christina: I am sorry, we will not be able to add this item along with this order, as the order has already been processed and sent to the warehouse. I am really sorry for the inconvenience caused in this regard.

Me: Can you place the order separately and apply the 10 percent discount?

Christina: I am sorry to say that the 10 percent discount has been already applied for the order you have already placed.

Me: Is there anyone that can help me? I placed the order less than twenty-four hours ago... and several other orders in the past for several thousands of dollars.

Christina: Due to our commitment to our customers, we try to process orders quickly. Once the checkout process is completed our warehouse is immediately notified to pack the order for shipment. Hence, we are unable to make any changes.

Me: So can you just please give me the 10 percent discount?

Christina: We regret any inconvenience that this may cause you. I'm sorry to say that the 10 percent discount has already been applied to the order number 28017716. I'd like to inform you that the discount and coupon amounts can only be used for one order. I apologize for any inconvenience this may cause to you.

Me: I certainly understand what you are describing, regarding the application of the discount to the previous order. But I would add a human element to this and trust that the customer just forgot to add the item to the cart and checked out before he could add it... It's not everyday that someone just wakes up and says I want to make a large purchase (like a TV). I forgot to add it to the cart last night.... As you can see, I have placed a few orders within the last week alone and several over the course of the year, hence I am a regular customer who likes to shop at Surplus Specialists.

Christina: I certainly understand your concern. What I can do for you is... If you would place the order right now, I will give you a free shipping for the order.

Me: Christina, I certainly appreciate the effort... Perhaps there is someone who can make the decision to provide a 10 percent discount for this order?

Christina: Since you have been a valuable customer to us, the maximum I can do for you is to issue a $10 coupon to your account, and you can place the order. May I go ahead and issue the coupon for you?

Me: Christina thanks for your help. But I am not willing to continue to do business with a company who does not realize that a customer made a mistake by not BUYING MORE. Checkout on this order was less than twenty-four hours ago and you will not allow me to use the 10 percent discount (that was applied to my account by Surplus Specialists because the last ordering process was a sheer disaster). Why would you want to push a customer away when he simply wants to buy more on an order... and add a TV? Perhaps you can secure a supervisor for me? I would really appreciate it. Though I realize that what you are doing is what is within your power.

Christina: Please stay online while I check what can be done for you.

Me: Thanks, Christina.

Christina: Thank you for staying online. I really appreciate your patience.

Me: No problem.

Christina: Michael, we strive to make sure that the only thing better than the prices at Surplus Specialists is the value we place on customer satisfaction. I have issued a 10 percent discount to your account. This will apply to your next order. You can go ahead and place the order. Customer satisfaction is our number one goal and we will make sure that such incidents do not occur again. Is there anything else that I can help you with today?

Me: Christina, I really appreciate your focus on this. I am placing the order now. Rest assured I will continue to tell my clients, colleagues, and friends about the Surplus Specialists experience.

Christina: Thank you so much. Thank you for contacting us. I would really appreciate it if you could take a moment to fill out a short survey at the end of this chat. Just click the "close" button on the chat window, and the exit survey will come up. Thanks. Thank you again for visiting Surplus Specialists. Have a great day! Bye, take care.

Chat session has been terminated by the customer service representative.

From what you read in the above scenario, write about the customer service experience from each person's point of view:

Christina: _____

Customer: _____

Manager: _____

Would you patronize this business again based on what you saw here? Why or why not? _____

_____

What would you do to change it to more of a World-Class Customer Service experience? _____

_____

It is very easy to become complacent with our customer service practices. What worked last year might not work this year, as can be seen with the fuel shortage story we discussed in Fresh Step 4. Employees who were positioned to provide a World-Class customer service experience may no longer have the confidence or tools to provide the same level of service today. It behooves us to constantly review our customer experience to ensure that the organization's expectations are aligned with what's actually delivered by the Frontline Employee.

Existing and new competition should still be viewed as a threat. Knowing this, your organization must constantly focus on beating the competition when it comes to providing a better level of customer service. I am sure very few people imagined that Starbucks could have taken the coffee business to the astounding level it has over the last decade.

And even fewer people would have thought that customers were willing to pay so much for the World-Class customer service experience that Starbucks has sought to create and deliver—and when it lags in delivering, it is quick to revise its processes and procedures.

Relentless Focus should be in the World-Class customer experience through Fresh Customer Service. This goal must be a constant priority of your organization. It's likely a number of other competing initiatives will be distracting and cause confusion that could dilute the importance of this goal.

Your leadership team should be careful to explain that providing a World-Class experience through Fresh Customer Service will initially be kicked off as a goal, but will quickly transcend into a standard operating objective and be embedded into the permanent culture of the organization. After the leadership team has put it in this context, they can move on to explain the necessary actions to get there. The actions are: Side-by Side Walking, Smart Tasking, Make-it-Right Power, the What-If Arsenal, Bubble-Up Innovation, and Relentless Focus.

Temperature Check

Okay, time to step away from the book and into the kitchen! To see how well done your Relentless Focus process really is, take the time to research and answer these 6.5 questions about the state of Relentless Focus in your organization.

1. Is the customer experience the same no matter who is in charge?

2. Are there silos in your organization?

3. Who is responsible for focusing on the customer experience?

4. When was the last time you participated in a session where all functions of the organization were in the same room?

5. What is your role in delivering the customer experience?

6. Is your focus on the customer steady, persistent, and un-yielding 365 days a year?

6.5. What mechanisms are in place to keep your organization from losing focus on the customer?

Ideally, you will answer "Yes" to questions 1 and 6, "No" to question 2, "Everybody" to question 3, and have recently participated in a session where all functions of the organization were in the same room. And of course, you should play a major role in delivering the customer experience (remember the proper answer to question 3!) and have strong, failsafe mechanisms in place to make sure your organization doesn't lose its focus on the customer.

If your results are similar to these, you have a well-done Relentless Focus process that should keep employees and customers alike happy and well-fed. Otherwise, double-check your oven thermometer and cook out some more of the red in your Relentless Focus!

Remember, promise what you can deliver. When you don't deliver on a promise you destroy your employees and customers lose trust in you, resulting in a complete loss of integrity with both your people and your customers.

So if you promise a "good customer experience" make sure you consistently deliver it; otherwise your employees will lose faith in the company and find other jobs, as will the customers, who will find other providers of goods and services.

Also, a final note on mystery shopping—not every business has face-to-face interactions with its customers. These organizations can still perform mystery shopping. Make a phone call, shoot an email, or engage in a live chat like the aforementioned Surplus Specialists example. How easy is it for your mystery shoppers to purchase goods, return an item, obtain information, or have issues resolved? Also if you are a web or catalog retailer, your website or catalog is your frontline. How easy is it to navigate that frontline? Are the "aisles" clearly marked and well-lit? How convenient is the "checkout lane"? Is it easy to call for virtual help?

What's your Temperature? Relentless Focus

Temperature	Correct Response Rate	Explanation
Rare	0 correct Temperature Check responses	In the 19th century, both Germany and Italy were divided into numerous mini-kingdoms that constantly warred with each other and sought out their own best interests, without regard for the good of the people as a whole. In other words, they were slightly more cooperative than your organization's internal departments.
Medium Rare	1-2 correct Temperature Check responses	There is some rudimentary interdepartmental cooperation, but no clear company-wide focus on accomplishing tasks. Customer service? Doesn't another department handle that?
Medium	3-4 correct Temperature Check responses	Departments cooperate and everyone realizes that customer service is a universal responsibility. If only everyone acted upon that realization…
Medium Well	5-6 correct Temperature Check responses	Departments cooperate closely for the good of the customer, and, in turn, of the bottom line. Employees "get" that customer service is everyone's responsibility. Perhaps better follow-up, or some interdepartmental meetings, would take you to the well done stage.
Well Done	**6.5 correct Temperature Check responses**	All employees, from the boardroom to the front line, have a true relentless focus on delivering World Class customer service. Departments work together seamlessly in support of this mission and a network of support mechanisms, such as interdepartmental meetings, keeps relentless focus in place.

*Keep checking the temperature to make
sure you get to Well Done and stay there

Fresh Technologies

Many of the technologies highlighted in previous chapters can also be applied to your efforts to bring a Relentless Focus to your organization. For example, automated loyalty programs can help you get to "know" your customer by tracking their purchase wants and needs, and then to meet those wants and needs with individually targeted upsell and cross-sell promotions.

In addition, wireless networks can seamlessly connect an entire enterprise, helping to eliminate silos and link all parts of the business to the frontline. Business intelligence systems can help an organization keep abreast of developing problems, such as a contractor who consistently delivers substandard services and generates customer complaints. And if those complaints come in on a weekend when frontline managers don't want to be present in the store, wireless devices and the Internet make keeping them "on call" that much easier!

 **News Fresh**

In October of 2006, *Fortune Magazine* reported how Irene Rosenfeld, once the President of the North American sector of Kraft (the world's second-largest food company), left the company to pursue a CEO title elsewhere. After a brief stint running Pepsi-Co's Frito-Lay, she was wooed back by Kraft, who offered her that CEO promotion she had always wanted. Now she aims to be a more transformational leader.

"I learned the value of relentless growth," she told *Fortune* about her experience running a different company. Reporter Patricia Sellers adds, "Three months into her new job [as CEO at Kraft], Rosenfeld is trying to view Kraft the way an insider would.

After visiting 22 Kraft plants around the world, she announced a sweeping reorganization to hand more power to the company's line operators." Note the focus on the frontline—the company line operators!

 Take Out

1. Align all Fresh Customer Service activities throughout your organization, from top to bottom. Everyone in the organization is equally responsible for providing World-Class customer service, and needs to have an equal stake in any customer service process. Though the Frontline Employee is the person who actually interacts with the customer, don't place all the responsibility on the shoulders of the Frontline Employee, and don't place all the

decision-making power in the corporate office. Only when everyone is aligned and focused on the prescribed customer experience will it truly become a consistent and sustainable World-Class customer service experience.

2. Embed the principles and practices of Fresh Customer Service into your corporate culture. Fresh Customer Service should be taken into account when devising any corporate goal or strategy, even if it is not directly customer-facing. How does the way you operate your warehouse, or purchase materials, or keep your books, impact the frontline environment?

3. Avoid corporate silos at all costs. There is no way to ensure a relentless focus on Fresh Customer Service throughout your organization if different departments are isolated from each other and act in their own best interests without concern for the good of the company as a whole. The customer pays the bills for every employee in every department, so there is no excuse for lack of cooperation in providing Fresh Customer Service to ensure the bills continue to get paid.

Fresh Step 6.5
Now Just Make It Happen!

Fresh Appetizer:
Welcome to the Real World

Wow, you've made it through the book! Give yourself a pat on the back. You've read all you need to know about the Fresh Steps necessary to achieving Fresh Customer Service. You know how to perform Side-By-Side-Walking with the Frontline Employee, you know the importance of Smart Tasking, you know how to award Make-It-Right Power, and you know how to build a What-If Arsenal. You realize Bubble-Up Innovation needs to be generated from the bottom up (lest it fizzle out), and you know that without Relentless Focus you might as well go home and stop kidding yourself about boosting your organization's bottom line. So what's the deal with this half-chapter?

Not so fast, my friend—that's what this half-chapter means. The implementation of Fresh Customer Service rests in your hands. Don't let all these Fresh Steps go in vain—right now it's time for you to just make it happen.

Fresh Entrée:
Taste the Results of Fresh Customer Service

I'm often asked, "Michael, what's the deal with 6.5 steps? Why the half-chapter—don't you have anything to say at the conclusion of your book?"

Of course I have more to say, but enough of my talking! The "point 5" reminds you that although you've just finished reading this book, you are only part of the way to where you need to be to deliver a World-Class customer experience. Chapter 6.5 is all about you. You need to walk away and take action. Your work is not done until you act and take these ideas to work with you everyday. Only then is this book a complete seven chapters—and seven is the lucky number as well as the number signifying successful implementation of Fresh Customer Service!

This last half-chapter is the most critical step in achieving a World-Class customer service experience; it is the bonding agent, the glue that will connect all of the steps and make them stick. I will run through a couple of brief examples of real-life clients who implemented Fresh Customer Service and achieved dramatic results.

At a gas station retailer I worked for, I had a manager who reported directly to me. He was a good performer in the company, but always wanted to be an entrepreneur. I will call him "Stephen."

Stephen would always spend extra time after work observing me and asking questions, trying to understand what I did to be so successful in business. He took note of everything I told him.

After about a year-and-half of this mentor-mentee relationship, we both moved on to different jobs. Several years later, Stephen called to thank me. He had opened a franchise of a popular doughnut shop chain, and after only seven months he had been successful enough to open a second one. Both were top producers in the chain. The vice president of the organization had called to congratulate him on being a top franchise prospect in sales. He had another franchisor interested in him coming on board to open stores with them. Word had spread around town and anyone could see that he had a booming business.

Within the first five minutes of my phone conversation with Stephen, he said, "Michael, you taught me to take care of the Frontline Employees, they would take care of the customer, and the bottom line would take care of itself. I have operated the business with that in mind, and now I am successful."

From Day One, Stephen had focused on and empowered his Frontline Employees so they could provide World-Class customer service. He gave them all the tools they needed to deliver a first-rate customer experience. He has since opened three more franchises using the same process and philosophy.

As a result, the bottom line takes care of itself. Stephen has gone from making $50,000 a year to making $250,000 a year, and expects to open four or five stores a year for the next four to five years.

In another "real world" example, I once worked as a consultant with an operator of an independent retailing/manufacturing business. He had a negative six percent growth from the prior year. I spent one-and-a-half days focusing on the retail side of his business, which was an oil/lube shop and car wash combined with a food store. He sold a little bit of everything!

We worked on how to communicate the desired customer experience to the employees, equip them with the proper tools (including a method and process to upsell), and empower them to deliver the experience. We also spent a large part of the day redesigning the customer offer. As a result of our efforts, he took steps to get employees involved with the operation, doing things like greeting the customers and understanding their needs. He empowered employees to deliver World-Class customer service and in a written document outlined the steps they should take, including steps from the LEAP and Fresh Smile programs.

Eight months later, I saw him at a convention in Las Vegas. He ran up to me and excitedly told me about the 26 percent sales lift he had experienced in those eight short months.

Temperature Check

How do you know if you have properly prepared a complete 6.5-course Fresh Customer Service meal? It's too large a task to completely encapsulate in 6.5 brief bullet points, but let's quickly summarize the key recommendations from each chapter.

1. Have your senior managers (including the "top brass" such as CEOs and CFOs) truly lived a day in the life of the Frontline Employee, from punching in and putting on the uniform to sweeping up, shutting off the lights and locking the front door?

2. Are you constantly reviewing Frontline Employees' daily tasks, taking input from Frontline Employees and customers, and regularly updating those tasks to best reflect what is most important in providing World-Class Customer Service?

3. Are your Frontline Employees empowered to resolve customer problems quickly and to ensure customers are satisfied every time they visit your business? Does common sense trump "corporate policy"?

4. Do Frontline Employees have access to an arsenal of up-to-date tools and techniques that fosters consistently superb business-to-customer interaction?

5. Does innovation bubble up from the frontline throughout your organization, all the way to the corporate boardroom?

6. Have you eliminated organizational silos to enable a company-wide environment where all employees, from the frontline to the back office, are relentlessly focused on doing what it takes to provide a World-Class customer experience?

6.5 This final half-step is the most important. It is more of an overarching principle to keep at the forefront of your thoughts when performing all other Fresh Customer Service processes and activities. **Are you making the employee number one, and the customer number two?**

If you can honestly answer "Yes" to all those questions, and a whole-hearted and enthusiastic "Yes," rather than a half-hearted "Sort of" or "Most of the time" or "It really depends on the situation," then you have created a 6.5-course Fresh Customer Service banquet that is worthy of being served at any five-star restaurant in the world!

What's your Temperature? Now Just Make It Happen!

Temperature	Correct Response Rate	Explanation
Rare	0 correct Temperature Check responses	This was a really interesting book. I'm going to carefully ponder what I've learned and maybe I'll try to use some of it one of these days.
Medium Rare	1-2 correct Temperature Check responses	You're making a token effort to stay on top of what your Frontline Employees are doing and how it impacts the customer. Great. Have yourself a cookie; you earned it.
Medium	3-4 correct Temperature Check responses	You take feedback from Frontline Employees and customers, but probably haven't figured out how to improve your business based on what you learn.
Medium Well	5-6 correct Temperature Check responses	You're doing a thorough job of understanding what your Frontline Employees and customers are experiencing, have put mechanisms in place to act upon what you learn, and regularly review your operation. But you know you could still do better.
Well Done	**6.5 correct Temperature Check responses**	You have realized what it takes to achieve maximum results from a complete 6.5-step Fresh Customer Service program. Therefore, you consistently put the employee first, and the customer second. Congratulations! Now that you have fully implemented everything you have learned from this book, maybe it's time to pass it along to a friend —one who is not a direct competitor, of course!

*Keep checking the temperature to make sure you get to Well Done and stay there

T Fresh Technologies

I'd like to offer some closing insights on the fresh technologies we have highlighted in the earlier chapters. By no means do they constitute an exhaustive list of all the technologies you can use to create a World-Class customer experience, nor will every available technology be the right fit for every organization. Remember that the business should drive the technology, and the technology should never drive the business.

Simply put, the preceding Fresh Technologies section are designed to give you an idea of what is happening in the world of high tech that can help you maximize the performance of your Frontline Employees, which will in turn maximize your customers' satisfaction levels and your bottom line. Take some time to investigate what kinds of business technology systems are out there waiting to be implemented at your organization. High tech is one of the few industries that can say with 100 percent sincerity that there is something new happening every day!

Take Out

1. Remember that once you have studied and mastered the first 6 steps to Fresh Customer Service, it's time to Just Make It Happen! Unless you take everything you have learned out into the real world, this book will simply turn into one more dusty old reference guide you keep on your bookshelf to show visitors how much you care about customer service. Implement all 6.5 steps! Perform trial and error, collect feedback from Frontline Employees and customers, then go back and refine your efforts. Fresh Customer Service is not a theory; it's a fluid way of running your business every day.

2. Before following any of the Fresh Steps in this book you should first figure out what type of quantitative and qualitative results you are seeking. Quantitative results are "hard" results that can be measured precisely. For example, after successfully performing a Side-By-Side Walking exercise and acting upon the results, you may see a 12 percent increase in bottom-line profits. In contrast, qualitative results are "soft" results that cannot be summed up in neat facts and figures, but are nonetheless real. For example, as a result of Side-By-Side Walking, Frontline Employee attitudes toward senior management may improve. Both results are extremely important, and

you should tailor all Fresh Customer Service efforts toward obtaining them.

3. Make the employee number one, and the customer number two. I cannot repeat this mantra enough. Every single
recommendation I make in this book, and every successful customer service decision I have made in my career,
springs from this seemingly counter-intuitive strategy.
But think about it. Who is motivated to do a better job:
a person who is valued, equipped with the right tools,
empowered, listened to, and well cared for; or a person
who is taken for granted, ignored, powerless and abused?
Take care of your employees first and they will take care of
the customers and the bottom line will take care of itself.
Try it. I am truly confident that you'll like the results.

Final Thoughts

Armed with what you've just read, now is the time to equip and empower your Frontline Employees to deliver Fresh Customer Service and a unique World-Class customer service experience!

The Frontline Employee is the world-class chef who can take the provided ingredients and recipe instructions and create a World-Class customer service experience that customers will pay top dollar for. But you must enable your chefs to create a five-star entrée!

Firstly, you must involve and engage your Frontline Employees in all levels of cultivating the customer experience, from selecting the ingredients to contributing to the decisions, strategies, policies and procedures enacted by the "executive chefs" at your organization. Thus, the Frontline Employees will be better equipped and empowered to unleash their passion and enthusiasm to prepare and deliver the main entrée, a World-Class customer service experience.

Put simply, who is the best salesperson of a product or service? You guessed it—the person who fully understands and believes in the product or service and is equipped and empowered to deliver it as part of an overall World-Class customer service experience.

When customers are the recipients of this level of passion and enthusiasm of the Frontline Employee, they will be more apt to open their wallets for the main entrée, as well as appetizers, side dishes, and desserts, and to come back for more helpings. Not only will they pay top dollar for this experience, it will be framed and etched in their minds where it will be shared with their many friends, colleagues, and even strangers.

So take care of your "master chefs"—Frontline Employees—*first* by equipping and empowering them to develop a healthy and robust menu, as well as a set of strong, reliable ingredients—customer service tools and techniques—and let them help pick out the dishes that will be served to the customers with a garnish I call Fresh Customer Service. Go ahead, unleash your budding chefs and watch them take care of the customer while the bottom line takes care of itself. I will say it again, *bon appetit!*

Notes

Introduction

Page 1 "Research shows that…": Chris Denove and James D. Power IV, *Satisfaction: How Every Great Company Listens to the Voice of the Customer* (New York: Penguin Group, 2006).

Page 1 "Almost one in four people in a May 2006 AP-Ipsos poll…": *USA Today*, Poll: Americans like instant gratification: www.usatoday.com/news/bythenumbers/2006-05-28-poll-gratification; Ipsos/Associated Press Polls: http://www.ipsos-na.com/news/ap/.

Fresh Step 1

Page 31 "According to an Associated Press article…": Elizabeth M. Gillespie, Starbucks' Sales Slide on Frozen Drinks (Associated Press, August 2, 2006).

Page 47 "According to Chris Denove…": Chris Denove and James D. Power IV, *Satisfaction: How Every Great Company Listens to the Voice of the Customer* (New York: Penguin Group, 2006), 288 pp.

Page 47 "Furthermore, the *Wall Street Journal*…": Scott McCartney, "With More Cash in Hand, Airlines Are Splurging on Better Service for Passengers" (*The Wall Street Journal*, May 9, 2007).

Fresh Step 2

Page 67 "'Companies simply must solve the service puzzle...'": Accenture, The Customer Service Challenge: Creating the "Perfect" Customer Call, 2006.

Page 72 "An article in *E-Commerce Times* paraphrased Rollins...": Keith Regan, "Dell Founder Accepts Blame for Company's Recent Woes" (E-Commerce Times, September 13, 2006).

Fresh Step 3

Page 97 "The study cites that 80 percent of executives...": *Fortune Magazine*, Vol. 154 No. 2, July 24, 2006.

Page 97 "He believes that this unrelenting behavior...": Ibid.

Fresh Step 4

Page 113 "Accenture performed its second annual survey..." Accenture, The Customer Service Challenge: Creating the "Perfect" Customer Call, 2006: www.accenture.com/.../0/ ThePerfectCall2006CustomerServiceSurveyReport.pdf.

Page 113 "Furthermore, The White House Office of Consumer Affairs...": TARP (Technical Assistance Research Program), Consumer Complaint Handling in America: An Update Study, White House Office of Consumer Affairs, Washington, DC, 1986.

Page 114 "He continues to say, 'Seven out of 10 complaining customers…'": Art Weller, Tips for Curing Bad Customer Service, The Customer Service Manager (CSM) Group website 2004-2005: www.customerservicemanager. com/customer-service-tips-for-curing-bad-customer-service.htm.

Fresh Step 5

Page 136 "They are so captivated by their own vision…": Howard Schultz and Dori Jones Yang, *Pour Your Heart Into It: How Starbucks Built a Company One Cup at a Time* (New York: Hyperion, 1997).

Page 136 "It seemed to dilute the integrity…": Ibid.

Page 136 "That's 52 million (dollars) we would not have registered…": Ibid.

Fresh Step 6

Page 155 "One way of gaining team involvement…": Patrick Lencioni, *Silos, Politics, and Turf Wars: A Leadership Fable About Destroying the Barriers That Turn Colleagues Into Competitors* (Hoboken, N.J.: Jossey-Bass, 2006), 224 pages.

Page 176 "In October of 2006…": Patricia Sellers, "A Transformational Leader at Kraft," Fortune Magazine, October 16, 2006.

Acknowledgments

Searching deep into my DNA to unearth all of this content and put it onto paper has been a challenging and rewarding journey. I am extremely grateful for the push and tremendous support of those Frontline Employees with whom I have worked at a number of companies and organizations. My family, friends, colleagues, and a host of cheerleaders have planted fertile seeds in me and helped me blossom into the individual and successful professional I am today. What I have sought to do all my life and in this book is keep these seeds watered and producing life's fresh green crops.

More specifically, I'd like to thank my mom, Ella, who taught me to always have unwavering faith, confidence and tenacity. I continue to be grateful for her teachings. Beverly Malloy, one of my greatest supporters and critics, continues to remind me of my potential and challenges me to stretch and always reach farther. Anthony Caruth, a former Frontline Employee of mine and an artist who contributed Fresh Customer Service artwork, has been a sounding board for my 6.5 Fresh Steps and has listened to me for months to help me verbally flesh out this book's concepts.

Anthony captured my intellectual property and transposed it into some of the greatest customer service art around. Leia Bonilla, thank you for some amazing cartoons. Francisco O. Bennett, whom I initially contracted to design a logo for my company, I am sure had no idea that a simple two week project would expand into a working relationship that continues to this day. Francisco's unwavering commitment and long, hard-working hours have helped me to shape my brands, Fresh Results and Fresh Customer Service, into something that will benefit the world.

I'd also like to thank Willie & Dee Taylor- Jolley, who gave me the final push to enter the professional speaking arena. Juanell Teague, Melanie White, and James Huggins helped me polish my thoughts and make Fresh Customer Service a reality. Beverly Weidner has given me support for over two decades and took the time to read through Fresh Customer Service and give me feedback from a non-corporate perspective. My ten brothers and sisters, who taught me early-on how to catch more flies with honey, continue to hold me in high regards.

Thank you to Carolyn Holliday McKibbin and Paige Stover Hague of Acanthus Publishing for taking me and Fresh Customer Service on—and a special kudos to my editor, Carolyn, for quickly understanding my voice and keeping it alive throughout *Fresh Customer Service*. And a warm thank-you to my other editor, Daniel E. Berthiaume, who came aboard at a critical time when I was trying to figure out how I could give the reader more (I guess that's the customer service in my DNA speaking). Dan listened patiently as I spewed my new visions out at about 165 mph while helping to ensure that you could actually understand and digest what I was saying.

My ten champions—Chandan Sengupta, Brad Sutton, Lloyd Tuckman, Ezra Sweis, Adrian Mitchell, Dr. Joann White, Eric Gagnon, Fred Lindsey, Anthony Caruth, and Michael Leiblow—read the concept of Fresh Customer Service in its infancy and provided enormous feedback.

I am extremely lucky to have worked with thousands of Frontline Employees who have been willing to learn from me and teach me how to really deliver fresh customer service by focusing on the Frontline Employee. I have learned immensely from each experience. These individuals have helped me to shape and enhance my servant-leadership style of management. Even in hard times my Frontline Employees helped to remind me of the importance of staying focused on people (our frontline and customers).

I thank God for allowing me early on to realize and continue to practice my passion—people and fresh results.

And last, but by no means least, I want to extend a warm and fresh thank you to you, the reader. Thank you for coming along on this Fresh Customer Service journey. I hope you have extracted tangible and timely solutions that will help you lead your organization to greatness, to delivering World-Class customer service experience each and every time. I especially hope you have a renewed commitment to focusing on your most valuable asset, the Frontline Employees.

Receive my Free Newsletter

I trust that you extracted value from the book. To continue receiving fresh and valuable information, please join my Fresh Results network and receive my free 6.5 minutes of Fresh Results newsletter, updates/tips, special discounts on Michael's Products, and so much more. Just go to www.themichaeldbrown.com to sign up.

Welcome to a Fresh new world of Fresh Results...

Ordering and Speaking Information

Fresh Customer Service is available at
www.themichaeldbrown.com and at your favorite
bookstores. Please contact us for quantity discounts.

The book is also available to the book trade and educators
through all major wholesalers.

To book Michael for speaking and training engagements
please go to www.themichaeldbrown.com and submit a
request form.

© Dennis Voeltner

About the Author

As a successful professional speaker, coach, and trainer, Michael D. Brown draws upon his own life experiences and highly successful corporate career to deliver unprecedented results that enhance the bottom line. Michael has a BBA in Management from Jackson State University, holds an MBA in Global Management, and earned the honors of summa cum laude graduate. With 15 years of technical and functional leadership experience, Michael delivers his message on *Fresh Customer Service*® through keynotes, seminars, workshops, and executive retreats.

Born the seventh of ten siblings, Michael was faced with having to be a creative provider at an early age. When he was 15 years old, he began peddling candy and other sweets from a plastic container tucked into his backpack that could be easily displayed to student customers. What began as a small candy business generating about $40 a day blossomed into one that generated $300 to $400 a day and competed with the school's concession stand. To say the least, Michael's ability to drive results started very early in life.

Ambitious for success, hungry for professional growth, and driven to help others, Michael has built his core values of determination, ambition, and creativity on the lessons he learned early in life, such as in his candy business. Later on in his professional career, he focused on helping not-for-profit organizations, consulting for some and acting as board member and director for others.

Michael has worked with and advised a number of Fortune 100 companies, global teams, entrepreneurs, and non-profits on *Fresh* strategy development, implementation, execution, and follow-up. Michael has worked with a number of great companies, organizations and firms, including: Murphy Oil (The Wal-Mart Project), USF&G Insurance, BP, Wells Fargo Financial, San Francisco Foundation, Ford Foundation, Marriott, Amoco, Ralph & Kacoo's Seafood Restaurant, Wendy's International, along with a number of small independent business owners. He has spent the last ten years working with the fourth largest Fortune Global Company in the world. His most recent assignment was directly leading a team of eleven district managers and an organization of 138 operations with more than 1,000 Frontline Employees.

Throughout his career, Michael has been renowned for his fast improvement of the bottom line. He has taken companies that haven't grown or were flat to 26 to 75 percent growth, while reducing expenses by 11 to 32 percent. He has helped to double customer satisfaction indexes for dozens of businesses within 45 days, and in one instance, he achieved a 75 percent increase in store sales and a 40 percent reduction in store expense in six months, turning a dying, unprofitable operation into a profitable, sustainable one. In addition, Michael has organized, produced, and directed over one hundred successful events, meetings, and conferences.

In every aspect of his leadership, speaking, coaching and consultancy, Michael takes the time to understand either an organization's corporate goals or an individual's personal goals, weaving them into a sound plan for the future.